The
Gift
of
Presence

The
Gift
of
Presence

Stories that Celebrate Nurses
Serving in the Name of Christ

Edited by
DAVE & NETA JACKSON
BETH LANDIS

HERALD PRESS
Scottdale, Pennsylvania
Waterloo, Ontario

Library of Congress Cataloging-in-Publication Data
The Gift of presence : stories that celebrate nurses serving in the
name of Christ / Dave and Neta Jackson and Beth Landis, editors.
   p. cm.
   ISBN 0-8361-3566-0
   1. Mennonite nurses—United States—Biography. 2. Missionaries,
Medical—United States—Biography. I. Jackson, Dave. II. Jackson,
Neta. III. Landis, Beth, 1957-
RT34.G43   1991
610.69'5'092—dc20
[B]   91-19070
                                                              CIP

The paper used in this publication is recycled and meets the mini-
mum requirements of American National Standard for Information
Sciences—Permanence of Paper for Printed Library Materials, ANSI
Z39.48-1984.

Scripture quotations are from the *Holy Bible: New International
Version*. Copyright © 1973, 1978, 1984 International Bible Society.
Used by permission of Zondervan Bible Publishers.

This book was developed in cooperation with The Mennonite Nurses
Association, Box 818, Goshen, IN 46526.

The cover: The illustration is from a photo of Nestor Avila, a patient
from Ecuador with AIDS. He is shown with a nurse at St. Vincent's
Medical Center in New York. The photo was taken by Ansell Horn and
is used by permission of Impact Visuals.

THE GIFT OF PRESENCE
Copyright © 1991 by Herald Press, Scottdale, Pa. 15683
   Published simultaneously in Canada by Herald Press,
   Waterloo, Ont. N2L 6H7. All rights reserved.
Library of Congress Catalog Number: 91-19070
International Standard Book Number: 0-8361-3566-0
Printed in the United States of America
Book design and cover art by Gwen M. Stamm

1 2 3 4 5 6 7 8 9 10 97 96 95 94 93 92 91

To nurses everywhere
who give of themselves

Contents

Preface

This book commemorates the fifty-year anniversary in 1992 of Mennonite Nurses Association. We celebrate the nursing experiences of Mennonite nurses past and present with stories from around the world telling how they have served in the name of Christ.

The stories were gathered in several ways. Invitations were published in several periodicals. Storytelling evenings were scheduled in various communities across the United States and Canada. Many individuals were contacted to submit anecdotes and memories of memorable patients, humorous incidents, touching moments, caring acts, and difficult situations.

Stories were written or taped and sent to Dave and Neta Jackson, who served as editors. Additional stories will be published in Christian periodicals in 1992 to further celebrate the fiftieth anniversary of MNA.

We are especially grateful to the following persons for helping create this book:

- Ida Gross and Maude Swartzendruber for the original idea for the book in 1978.
- All the nurses who took the time and energy to write or tell their stories.
- Volunteer typists: Brenda Srof and Grant Martin.
- Frances Bontrager Greaser for spending hours in the archives to piece together the history of MNA.
- Reviewers: Helen Alderfer, who gave valuable counsel in improving the book's appeal to persons who aren't nurses. Janis Miller, who is concerned about compassion as much

as nursing theory and the future of nursing. Patricia Shoemaker Yoder for sensitivity to detail related to nursing process and contemporary nursing issues. Schelli Weaver, who brought the perspective of a high school student with an interest in nursing. Ida Gross, who thoughtfully read and reread each story and called several authors to learn more about them and their story.

- Dave and Neta Jackson, for their superb editing. The style and personality of each writer was left intact, but the flow of words and ideas was enhanced.
- S. David Garber of Herald Press, who gave some initial direction as we struggled with the dream of undertaking a book project.
- Miller-Erb Nursing Development Fund, for a grant toward expenses.

As a member of the executive committee of Mennonite Nurses Association, I coordinated the project and collection of stories. It was my pleasure to read each story and accompanying notes and letters as they arrived.

Nurses, Christian nurses, Mennonite nurses, affect the lives of the people they serve. The stories in this book are about that impact on those real people. Some stories are humorous, some heroic, some amazing. They come from many countries and show such a penchant for the unusual that one must agree that truth *is* sometimes stranger than fiction. Truly, nursing "at the end of the road" requires a lot of creativity and courage.

All stories were written by registered nurses unless otherwise indicated. Read them to learn more about nurses and nursing. Be inspired to go about your work the next day with more respect. Take extra time, and minister more diligently to others.

—Beth Landis, Mennonite Nurses Association
Executive Committee, Goshen, Indiana

The
Gift
of
Presence

Night Shift

by Nancy Burkey

Nancy Burkey lives in Lebanon, Oregon. She has worked twenty years on the night shift as a staff and charge nurse for a small rural hospital. She has also done camp nursing and worked in blood banks.

The sprawling complex lies ahead of me in the dark night. Lights gleam from the long corridors and through many windows, giving the appearance of a miniature city. This "city" never sleeps. It is open twenty-four hours a day.

I bring my light blue Buick to a halt at 10:40 p.m. near the back entrance of the hospital. The landscaped lawn is shadowed, and large floodlights beam streaks of light across the concrete walks.

"Dear Lord, grant me the strength for this night's work. Grant me clarity of mind as I take care of the sick. Grant me wisdom and help me to be sensitive to the one who is especially in need of my service. May I show compassion and be gentle to all I meet tonight."

With this prayer I begin my duties.

✢ ✢ ✢

In Room 215 is Jack, a huge burly man with tattoos on both

arms and one of a woman's lips on his chest. He is not asleep. He is pacing and complaining about the cigarette fumes filtering into his room. He has chronic obstructive pulmonary disease and is short of breath. He is demanding a room change immediately.

I arrange the transfer, moving him and his belongings to another room at the far end of the hall. I put him in a room with Clarence, a quiet, nonsmoker who is having heart problems.

I leave, then look back. Clarence's call light is on. I return. "Could you ask this new guy to quiet down so I can sleep?"

I continue my rounds. From Room 220 I hear a faint, "Help me. Help me."

Deidre is old, frail, and curled up in a fetal position. She does not know where she is. Blood is spurting from her intravenous tube. The tubing is disconnected and hanging over the side rail. I connect and restart the IV then change the bed linen.

"Just go to sleep now, Deidre. Everything will be okay." I hope I'm right.

I look in on Gigi. The little one-year-old with atelectasis is sleeping peacefully in her crib with her tiny hand positioned across her face. She has been emotionally deprived and abused. Recently she picked at her eye in frustration until she became blind. I wonder what will happen to her tiny life as she grows into adolescence and adulthood. Will there be anyone to love her or meet her emotional needs?

Stormy, a thirteen-year-old, is sitting up in bed, staring into space. "Is there anything you need?"

She shakes her head. Stormy overdosed on drugs and tried to commit suicide. Her mother's newest boyfriend had been sexually abusing her. Tonight she's safe. I hope we can arrange an alternate living situation before she goes home.

As I step into the hall, the emergency room cart moves past. I follow it to settle Rob in a bed for a few days of observation.

"I think I have AIDS, and I can't eat any more," he says.

There are needle tracks up and down both arms, but he's got a friend, a haggard-looking kid who stands in the corner with greasy, long hair and dirty tennis shoes.

Rob pleads, "Can he stay with me? I can't handle this all by myself."

Back in the hall, the call lights seem to be on above every other door. Is no one sleeping? Or is it just that the night brings patients face to face with their illness? Pain tolerance lessens, and nervous tension escalates. I must provide a link between the night's fears and the morning light.

In Room 240 is Thomas, an eighty-six-year-old man. I do a nursing assessment. He's talkative and wants to tell me detailed stories of his relatives. I notice a half-eaten brownie wrapped in cellophane on the floor so I tidy up and throw it in the newly lined wastebasket. On I go. Nearly 3:00 a.m.—and I haven't taken a break yet.

What? The call light over 240 is back on? "Thomas, what do you want now?"

"Where's my chew?"

"You're what?"

"My chew, my tobaccee! I've been chewing for over sixty years. Still got my teeth, so I still got more chewin' to do."

"Oh. I thought it was a half-eaten brownie. I didn't think you wanted it, so I . . . ." I lean over and neatly fish it out of the wastebasket without Thomas noticing.

"Here. Here you go," I say. After sixty years, what could I say about the perils of tobacco chewing that would mean anything? Thomas is pleased.

In Room 245 is a lady named Josephine. She is confused, distraught, and trying to get out of bed. Crash, bang, the water pitcher falls to the floor. The splash makes long wet streaks on the carpet.

"Josephine," I say quietly.

Her glazed eyes stare at me. She needs her medication. After

15

I administer it, she begins to calm down. Her children—who didn't know what to do when she was so upset—graciously thank me. Their gratitude is a burst of light in the early morning darkness.

Next door ninety-six-year-old Elizabeth waits for someone to answer her light. She is unable to keep food down. It has been that way for days. Surgery is a last resort for an esophageal blockage. She will have it in the morning. She looks scared.

"Would you like me to pray with you?" I ask.

"Yes. Oh please do. I'm not afraid to die. I've known the Lord as my Savior for many years, but. . . ." She can't put more into words.

I pray, then I say, "Do you know John 14:1?"

"I think I do."

"Say it after me. 'Do not let your heart be troubled.' "

" 'Do not let your heart be troubled.' "

" 'Trust in God; trust also in me.' "

" 'Trust in God; trust also in me.' "

"Do you know who said that?" I ask.

Her eyes are closing. "Uh-hum. My Jesus did." And she is asleep.

Back at the nurses station, I sit on the corner of the desk and gaze out the window at the horizon. There's a jagged, lemon-colored streak painted across the tops of the far hills. The night is passing. I think of another verse, the one that keeps me going. "The King will reply, 'I tell you the truth, whatever you did for one of the least of these . . . you did for me.' "

I look down the hall. There are no more call lights.

Give Me a Break, God!

by Brenda Barkman as told to Jolyn Braun

*Brenda Barkman lives in Venezuela. She served three years in
Paraguay with the Evangelical Mennonite Conference. She has
furthered her education by studying tropical diseases.*

*Jolyn Braun lives in Landmark, Manitoba. She spent one year
in Venezuela teaching for New Tribes Mission. She was an
English major in college and does some free-lance writing.*

Wriggling cautiously, I try to inch over. *Oh, this is impossible*, I
think in frustration. Why won't the hammock quit swinging?
My sweat glued-on blouse yanks at my skin as I try to keep my
frosted tea upright while my body searches for relaxation on
this coarsely woven, seemingly sea-tossed piece of comfort fur-
niture. My inherent perfectionism, blown into full bloom by my
aching back, yearns for the illusion of ultimate peace.

"Oh brother," I mumble in despair, "does no one care that I
need a break?"

My love for God and my love of nursing had tugged at me
until recently I found myself in the Chaco, Paraguay, caring for
Lengua Indians. Fulfilling, yes. But how I wish I could with one
hefty kick send these early adjustments soaring.

Is God really here? I struggle inside. If God is here, in control,
and honored by my service, why doesn't God do something
about the difficulties I encounter?

A patient in pain blabbers, *"Asqueje coo."* Due to my linguistic inadequacy, we resort to hand communication and facial gestures. How idiotic I feel as we waste valuable time stumbling around. Finally I grasp the problem and can take help.

I dare you to drive on our dirt roads! During the dry season, huge billows of dark dust are produced by any traveling vehicle. Clinging relentlessly to the rear fender, the boiling cloud of dust rolls and tumbles and mushrooms into formidable gray-black fog.

Dangerous as this poor visibility makes our transportation, the wet season alternative is no better. With no gravel on the roads to counteract the effect of the moisture, all earth seems transformed into grease as we swerve and skid and slide through the mire.

Whenever our small clinic can't cope with a serious situation, Betty, my co-worker, and I race the thirty miles to the medical center at Yalve Sanga. The traveling conditions chain our record down to one hour at best.

Bang! Bang, bang! My breather is interrupted by someone at the door. Betty and I almost bump heads as we meet there.

All my nursing instincts—concern, pity, "let's do something to help" feelings—surge through me as a pair of young parents hand over their unconscious baby. Her breathing is difficult. The fontanel—the soft spot on the baby's head—is bulging and hard. Suspecting meningitis, we give injections for fever and an antibiotic.

"We better get her to Yalve Sanga," Betty notes in concern. As she strides briskly to the radio, I scurry out and bring the truck around.

"Oh God," I pray silently as I settle the Indian pair with their child on the sheepskin blankets in the truck box, "Please let us make it to the medical center in time. Show me that you are here and that you care."

Betty climbs behind the wheel as I hop in. She shifts once,

then again, snaps on the headlights in the descending dusk, and the clinic is out of sight.

In our state of emergency, our progress reminds me of the famous turtle. But hopefully we also will win this race.

An oncoming car passes us, leaving huge whirlwinds of dust in our path. We're reduced to a crawl as we carefully forge our way through. Minutes pass before we can increase our speed.

"God," I plead again and again, "reach down and touch that baby with your healing hand. Please let her live till we reach Yalve Sanga."

The Spirit responds. Soon the phrase, "Fix our eyes on Jesus . . . the author and perfecter of our faith," from Hebrews 12:2 is swirling through my thoughts. Peace pours into the cab. Confident, I flash Betty an encouraging smile. She presses harder on the accelerator, challenging our trusty truck to ever greater feats.

Soon Yalve Sanga's outlying farmsteads are whizzing past. But fists pounding on our cab window jolt us. Betty halts the truck.

"No hay caso, se fallicio," the husband shouts choppily. Betty understands the dismal words better than I, but one glance at the parents' dazed eyes is meaningful enough. Their ten-month-old girl is dead.

A careful examination at the medical center confirms it: "Dead."

"God, how could you?" My fists clench tight till my knuckles pop white as we chug home. "Are you even there?"

Despair overwhelms me.

And the concept of "perfected faith" eludes me entirely as I stare blankly out the window the next morning. The horse and buggy carrying the girl's body rolls past. Tears blur my vision.

After a seeming century of minutes, the phrase, "Fix our eyes on Jesus," enters my doubts. What could it mean? Tentatively, I reach out and touch it. Then I grab hard—in my desperation

19

that phrase promises hope. Soon I am chanting it over and over. "Fix our eyes on Jesus. *Fix our eyes on Jesus.*"

"Can't God be trusted!" I ask myself. "Or must *I* oversee everything?"

I think of Job. And of how he was brought face to face with the unfathomable mysteries of God. After all, I once again realize, if I as a mere human could fully understand God, how superior would God really be?

Peace fills me.

It doesn't arrive in a gushing flood. It comes in small installments, one after the other, until it grows into an awesome feeling of contentment. Before God's all-knowing love, I can lay down my frustrations, my life. I can let God be God.

So Lengua friends, foreign lingo, and swirling dust—make way! I might be here to stay.

Multipurpose Contraceptives

by Anne Warkentin Dyck

Anne Warkentin Dyck lives in Swift Current, Saskatchewan. She worked in Indonesia for twenty years with Mennonite Central Committee. Her focus was on midwifery, giving care in clinics, and operating room nursing. Since then she has worked in a senior citizen's home and chronic care hospital. She volunteers time with an Alzheimer's disease support group.

In the 1950s and 1960s in Indonesia, two of the commodities our hospital received from the Mennonite Central Committee were shipments of canned beef in sturdy cardboard boxes and various pharmaceutical samples in steel drums. The empty cardboard boxes were ideal for sorting the contents of the drums. These boxes were then labeled and neatly stacked on the spare wooden, double bed in my large bedroom. So well were they organized that I could find what I wanted in the dark. Or so I thought!

Then came the evening when our worker, Abraham, complained of a sore knee. After careful examination, Glenn Hoffman, our doctor, discovered no serious injury and began wrapping Abraham's knee in an elastic bandage. But soon Abraham protested that his knee wouldn't get better if it didn't have medicine. Patiently, Glenn agreed and asked me to get some ointment while he unwrapped the bandage.

We had no electricity, and I was saving my flashlight batteries in case I needed them for home deliveries. So I went after the Ben Gay (for rheumatic pains) in the dark. I grabbed a tube, came out, and handed it to Glenn. He glanced at it, said, "Sure, this will do," and squeezed a considerable amount on Abraham's knee.

Watching him trying to rub it in and the way it "squished" between his fingers rather than absorb into the skin as the pain ointment normally would, I sensed something strange. I looked at the tube in the light. It said, "contraceptive jelly."

Chris Yoder (an agricultural co-worker) walked in right then. I handed him the tube without comment and pointed to the doctor and patient. Chris looked at the tube and then at Glenn and said, "Hoffman, I think you're a quack."

A little taken aback, Glenn said, "Yoder, you get out of here." Then in Indonesian, "This feels better, doesn't it, Abraham?"

All the while I remained straight-faced and professional while the doctor rubbed away on poor Abraham's knee.

Finally, Chris shook his head again, "I tell you, Glenn, I'm going to have to report you to MCC so you won't get a job when you get home." (Glenn was about at the end of his term.)

Then Glenn said in Indonesian, "Your knee will feel better tomorrow." And in English he said, "Yoder, just go away and let me practice medicine."

Finally, somehow, the jelly was all rubbed in (or went somewhere!), the bandage was applied, and the happy patient retired to bed. Then we showed Glenn the label on the tube and all had a good laugh.

The next morning, however, we all witnessed one of those little miracles of modern medicine: Abraham's knee was completely well.

✦ ✦ ✦

Several years later, on the island of Java, I was working in a clinic. The people we served were poor. Having trouble feeding their large families, some came to the clinic asking for help with birth control. This was a politically volatile time, however; the president had said his country didn't need family planning. Anyone involved in promoting it, he had announced, could get into trouble.

We proceeded with caution—both because we had few resources and also not to attract government attention. Then one day we received a telegram from CWS (Church World Service) in Jakarta asking us if we could use some "EMKO fungicide." Knowing that EMKO was a contraceptive foam, not a fungicide, we recognized the care they were taking in making the offer.

One of our doctors suggested asking for 500 bottles, but another doctor, more involved with family planning, said, "Why not just ask for as much as they can give us?" So we did.

Some days later I was called out of a meeting to help an MCC worker figure out where to put the truckload of "stuff" that had just arrived. Did it need a rat-proof place or could it go in an older warehouse? The bill of lading said, "EMKO fungicide."

As we were discussing this the truck driver, who did not understand English, stepped forward timidly and volunteered, "Excuse me please, but if you are talking about my load, you should know my friend is about half an hour behind me with a similar load."

So CWS had shifted onto us some of their desire not to be caught with all that contraceptive. But had we not asked for it? Anyway, there was less chance of our getting into trouble in the "boonies" than for them in the capital city. But what would we do with it all?

A few months later, as we walked into church for the Christmas program, we saw our first Indonesian Christmas tree with "imitation snow." It took us only a few seconds to recognize the big blobs of white stuff! Later when the candles were lit, the blobs glistened in the flickering lights, making an interesting effect. Not like snow on a tree, exactly, but interesting, neverthe-less.

Somehow the word got out about our beautiful Christmas tree. The next December we got several requests from Christmas program committees for "EMKO snow" for their trees.

The government fell soon after this, so we were free to offer our more-than-abundant supply of EMKO for its intended use!

The Arrival of Penicillin

by Grace M. Lehman

Grace M. Lehman lives in Kidron, Ohio. She worked as a staff nurse in La Junta, Colorado, as her first job. Then she moved to Ohio and worked as a staff nurse and supervisor in obstetrics.

Laura Johnston was an attractive young woman, twenty-three years of age and the mother of a nine-month-old daughter, Karly. I first met Laura in La Junta, Colorado, in early 1944, during one morning when the nursing staff and students took time to read a portion of Scripture to patients. For the next six weeks I was assigned to care for Laura.

Her lengthy stay was the result of an infection of the bone marrow of her right thigh bone. She stayed in the hospital nearly three months, most of the time in bed. Her disease caused an open lesion from which oozed infectious drainage. Her care required strict isolation, which added an extra burden to an already heavy assignment.

The only treatment and medications at that time were analgesics (aspirin and codeine), sedatives, regular saline irrigation of the lesion every four hours with a change of dressings as needed, intravenous solutions of glucose to counteract dehydration, and total bed rest. The infection also caused unusual depression and took its toll on her normally pleasant disposition.

In early 1944, sulfa was the only drug available for infections, but it was ineffective in fighting osteomyelitis, Laura's disease. One day her physician, Dr. Guy Colonge, suddenly announced the possibility of securing a new drug known as an *antibiotic*. The FDA had just approved it. It was called "penicillin." It turned out that Dr. Colonge had been negotiating for many weeks to obtain the drug specifically to fight Laura's disease.

The atmosphere on the medical unit was tense as patient, doctor, and staff anticipated its arrival. Laura's disease was spreading ever so slowly but surely. If the penicillin did not arrive in time, and if it did not work, the only option was to amputate her leg.

In a few weeks, Dr. Colonge told us that the antibiotic was on the way from New York City to Denver and by courier from Denver to La Junta. The medication came in individual glass vials of one million units per dose. Laura was given medication every twelve hours.

In only a few days the miracle of penicillin became obvious. The first indication was a lowered body temperature, which had been consistently at 101 to 103 degrees. Next came the dwindling drainage from the lesion, then the gradual increase in strength from bed rest to chair to walking again.

I was present at her discharge. And when I left La Junta, Laura and her husband and small daughter were adjusting successfully to normal homelife.

History in the Making

by Lois Kuhns Ramseyer

Lois Kuhns Ramseyer lives in Goshen, Indiana. She worked as a staff and head nurse of labor and birth, director of nursing of a hospital in Nebraska, and as a staff nurse in extended care facilities in Indiana. She served in Korea with Mennonite Central Committee as a nurse consultant for a general hospital and a children's hospital following the Korean War.

It was February 11, 1944, and the last month of our "probie" (probation) days at La Junta Mennonite School of Nursing. Next month we would be full-fledged freshmen nurses! Sixteen pairs of eyes and ears focused on the instructor as she was showing for the third time the setup for an intravenous infusion. (Only physicians *started* IVs at that time.)

We were in the demonstration room on the first floor of the hospital. Miss Wilma Graber had chosen one of the class members to be the "patient" and another to assist her in the procedure.

The IV tray was placed on the bedside table, the "patient" was reassured and made comfortable, the arm board was applied. Four strips of tape were cut and hung where they could be reached quickly and easily, the rubber tubing tourniquet was slipped under the patient's arm just above the elbow, and the IV pole with the suspended bottle of IV fluid was in place.

Miss Graber went through the whole sequence, step by step. We all knew that the very next time we encountered this procedure would be at a real patient's bedside in a real situation! Three times with supervision . . . then we were on our own!

At the end of the class period Miss Graber came to me with her little black book of records. She said, "Miss Kuhns, this afternoon you will be assisting Dr. Guy Colonge with an IV in Room 227. The patient is Mrs. Laura Johnston who has osteomyelitis of the right femur and apparently is getting no better. Dr. Colonge wants to try the new drug, penicillin, on her! I'll meet you at one o'clock outside Room 227 and will help you set up."

Oh, help! I silently prayed to God, but to Miss Graber I replied, "I'll be there!"

I scarcely touched my food that noon meal. My classmates at our table were chatting, laughing, and enjoying their food. But I could only eat anxious thoughts—and indigestion set in. I left the table early and hurried to a small closet that I had discovered was seldom entered by anyone. There in the dark with the door closed I prayed, "Dear God, help me to keep my senses and do exactly as we've been shown!"

When I left the closet a couple minutes later, I felt easier in my mind—and my stomach. I somehow knew that God would also be in Room 227 that afternoon.

Mrs. Johnston was a young mother and very ill. She had been a patient in the hospital for some time, and we all had been told of her situation. If she did not get help soon for her infection, her leg would have to be amputated to save her life.

Dr. Colonge had made some important decisions and phone calls lately concerning the new drug, penicillin, which we had been hearing so much about. I remember thinking, *How could something moldy ever help cure anyone?*

Just that morning the precious package had arrived by special courier from Denver. It had been flown there from New

York. Upon its arrival Dr. Colonge was notified. He quickly took possession of it. The whole hospital was buzzing with the news of penicillin being brought into our midst.

At one o'clock sharp I was waiting at the door of 227. In just a few moments Miss Graber came walking up, smiling and saying, "Ready?"

Together we went to pick up the IV tray. On the way Miss Graber said, "I didn't tell you this morning that Dr. Colonge is rather nervous about this first use of penicillin, so everything must go well!"

Miss Graber must have sensed some tenseness rising in me because she quickly added, "Now if you do just as you've been taught, everything *will* go well! And I'll be there to help if needed."

With these reassuring words, I began to relax and even to feel glad that I was the one to help in this first use of penicillin.

Miss Graber and I entered Room 227, introduced ourselves to Mrs. Johnston, and told her of our mission. She was glad because for several weeks she had been looking forward to this hour. Dr. Colonge had told her that penicillin was her only hope, so she could hardly wait to get started.

I proceeded to set up. I was behind the bed against the far wall, with scarcely room enough for me, the table, the IV pole, and the doctor. It was 1:15 p.m.

In the meantime, the room began to fill with observers—students, nurses, and doctors, all wanting to witness the injection of this new miracle drug. There was a mysterious and hushed feeling pervading the room, as all waited for Dr. Colonge to arrive.

Among those in the room, standing at the foot of the bed, was young Dr. Richard Davis. Dr. Davis loved to tease the nurses, especially the students. Beside him stood Dr. R. S. Johnston, Sr., who *never* jested and was always sedate and proper.

At 1:20 p.m., in walked Dr. Colonge with a small vial in his hand. Seeming not to even see the audience, he went straight to the back side of the bed where I had set up for him.

My heart beat hard with the tension. "Dear God, please help me. Help Dr. Colonge and help Mrs. Johnston. And *please* don't let me blow it!"

Dr. Colonge cleansed the top of the small bottle, mixed its precious contents with sterile H_2O, and added it to the larger IV bottle.

At that precise moment, someone came in and called Miss Graber away. She whispered, "I'll be back." My frantic prayer went up, "I *really* need you now, Lord!"

"Tighten the tourniquet," mumbled Dr. Colonge. I thought I heard him right, but Dr. Colonge had a way of running his words together. I cast a quick glance for Miss Graber, but she had gone. So I cautiously tightened the tourniquet.

Dr. Colonge cleansed the site of injection, let the air bubbles escape from the tubing, then skillfully inserted the needle into the vein.

I watched for the blood to return into the tubing, then I carefully released the tourniquet. I did everything just as we'd been taught, but I hadn't waited for Dr. Colonge to tell me to release the tourniquet.

"No! Now what'd you do that for?" sputtered Dr. Colonge, and he actually slapped at my hand. Then, apparently not wanting to make any more of the situation, he said, "Oh never mind! It's all right."

The stillness and closeness in that room was suffocating. I didn't dare look up—it seemed to me that every eye must be on me and my blunder. Actually, everyone was probably far more interested in watching Mrs. Johnston's face for any reaction to the medication. But I felt like the center of attention and wanted only to get out of there for some fresh air.

I finally glanced up. Who should catch my eye but Dr. Davis. But instead of an *Aha, now see what you've done!* look, he winked a message to me that seemed to say, *Don't worry. You did all right!*

Gradually the room began to empty. When Dr. Colonge got the drip regulated to his liking, and had taped the tubing securely, he too left . . . to my utmost relief.

I stood there. It seemed like I was glued to the floor. Finally I gathered my wits together and *forced* my legs to move. Slowly I picked up the tray items, put things in order in the room, and left. Grace Lehman, Mrs. Johnston's nurse, remained with her.

Outside the door, I bumped into Miss Graber, who was just returning.

"I knew you could do it!" she said.

But she never knew just how much I had suffered in the process. I replied, "Oh, I guess it went all right." To myself I breathed a prayer of thanks to God for being there.

Well, the great new drug worked its miracle. Mrs. Johnston *did* recover. And so did I. I tried to stay clear of Dr. Colonge after that and was successful for a few weeks. Then I became the first in my class to be assigned to operating room education and experience. And guess what, my very first "scrub" was to help Dr. Colonge.

But I remembered Dr. Davis' twinkle of encouragement in 227, saying, "Don't worry! You did all right!" And I remembered too how my heavenly Father had been with me in that hard hour. I took fresh courage, and everything *did* go well. I loved my operating room education—even when assisting Dr. Colonge. I understand now that he was just as nervous and tense as I was that day when *we* made a bit of history in La Junta Hospital and for Mrs. Johnston.

Caring for an Outlaw

by Ruth Sollenberger Mellott

Ruth Sollenberger Mellott lives in McConnellsburg, Pennsylvania. She worked in Philadelphia hospitals as a staff and private duty nurse. She also worked as a public health nurse for the state of Pennsylvania.

During the mid-1930s, I was doing general-duty bedside nursing in a well-known hospital in Philadelphia. My shift was night duty on a men's ward. It was during the era of John Dillinger, "public enemy number one," the outlaw who made all the headlines in the newspapers. Dillinger was finally identified going into a theater in Chicago by a lady wearing a red hat.

When I reported for duty one evening at 7:00 p.m. (we worked twelve-hour shifts), I was told that a new patient was on the unit. He was in a private room and would be guarded by an armed policeman at all times. He had been shot and needed medical treatment. "He's a dangerous outlaw, similar to Dillinger," I was told.

But to me he was always a gentleman and respected my profession. I couldn't have asked for a more friendly, courteous, and cooperative person. One time he opened up and talked a little about his life. He wasn't sure how he had gotten into his present state. He'd been raised in a parochial school but for some reason had become bitter. When he left school and was on his own, he got into the wrong company. Before long he was so involved with a criminal gang he was afraid he would be killed if he tried to get out.

He was only with us a few days, then was discharged.

Sometime later the night supervisor sent me a newspaper clipping. It said my notorious patient had been fatally shot. The paper report said, "Good riddance!"

I was just a small-town girl working in the big city with the Brethren In Christ Mission, but I wasn't so sure the death of my outlaw patient was such a good riddance after all.

Emergency

by F. Arline Zimmerman

F. Arline Zimmerman lives in New Holland, Pennsylvania. She spent twenty years as a school health nurse in Philadelphia. She worked three and a half years in Korea with Mennonite Central Committee and on assignments in India and Costa Rica.

There was a restlessness, a sadness, a grief in Philadelphia in 1968. Juvenile gang lords ruled the streets. High school students were recruited by offers they "could not refuse." They joined gangs called "The Stars," "Crowns," "Diamond Street Rattlers," "Chain Gangs." More than fifty gangs were known to be active by the police department. Gang members killed each other in frequent street fights or *rumbles*. Gang members carried guns in the schools and swaggered proudly in the halls.

Those who resisted recruitment peeked around corners before entering corridors. They spent much of their free time in the library or in the health room visiting the school nurse.

My school was Edison High.

One day at lunch, as I was filing health records, I heard hurried footsteps in the corridor. Looking up, I saw a student with blood spurting from his neck. He was flanked by two other students and followed by four big, burly, well-dressed men.

Later I learned the four men were plainclothes police officers and heard one say, "I've been a police officer for twenty years but never saw anything like the stabbing I saw today."

I dropped the health records and flew across the room as I mentally prepared my actions: *Pressure on the ruptured artery. But will pressure on the jugular dangerously deprive the brain of oxygen? Will pressure on the subclavian artery be effective?*

I pressed my thumb on the jugular and guided the student to the cot as I shouted orders to the escorts. "Call the ambulance. Then call his mother and tell her to go to Episcopal Hospital!"

"Call the Emergency Room at Episcopal Hospital and tell them that a student with severe bleeding will be arriving from the high school. Notify the principal."

I silently breathed a prayer as I reviewed my mental nursing care plan. *Since limited pressure can be applied, find a way to lower the boy's blood pressure,* I told myself.

I spoke calmly and softly to my patient. "We need to work together," I told him as he lay prone on the cot. "Pretend you are a wet leaf on a mossy log floating lazily down the stream."

The boy went limp. I could feel the pressure lower under my thumb as he relaxed. I kept the pressure on the jugular vein until the boy said, "I feel like I am going to pass out." I momentarily released the pressure and blood spurted. The escorts and other observers kept silent. The process of pressure, release, bleeding; pressure, release, bleeding went on. It continued until the ambulance crew arrived about ten minutes later.

The nurse with the ambulance crew continued the process until they arrived at the emergency room. The boy survived. He returned to classes a few days later at another school.

I will call the student James. I frequently wonder if James is grateful for life. Did he become a later victim of gang warfare on the streets of Philadelphia, or a victim of poverty?

More than twenty years have passed since James was a sophomore and refused to join a gang. I later discovered that he had been stabbed in the neck as he was peacefully eating lunch in the "supervised," crowded, school cafeteria. The weapon, a stiletto knife, was fortunately honed to the sharpness of a surgeon's scalpel. There was little if any crushing of the vessel wall. That reduced the risk of blood clots and obstruction of blood flow to the brain.

I felt the power of God ruling over the nurse-patient interaction that day in the spring of 1968. I believe witnesses also sensed the presence of our Lord in the room in that time of great distress at Edison High School in Philadelphia.

Saved by the Instructor

by Mary Smucker

Mary Smucker lives in Goshen, Indiana. She worked as an
office nurse, staff nurse on a medical unit, nursing instructor
for family health for Goshen College, and community educator
for the Red Cross. She spent one year in India with Mennonite
Board of Missions and worked in several areas including
operating room and nursing education.

We were "probies," short for nurses on probation. A thousand miles from my rural Ohio home, I was starting nurses'
education at La Junta Mennonite School of Nursing in Colorado.

We practiced procedures in our laboratory classroom. After
the demonstration bath on "Martha" the doll, we used classmates as models. Each student was supervised when she gave
her three first real patients morning care, including a bath.

Miss Nora Miller was our able, confident, veteran nurse instructor. At that time I wore a simple gown over my dress.
There was no uniform, no cap, and no white shoes or stock-
ings. I was eighteen and had been reminded by my classmates
that I was not only the youngest but naive as well.

The first patient assigned to me was the Catholic priest of a
Spanish congregation in La Junta. He was in the hospital with a
broken back. But when Miss Miller—dressed in a full uniform—

took me into the patient's room and introduced me, I met a
cold stare and a disgruntled patient.

Before I could get out basin and towels, he said, "I won't be
experimented on by some young girl off the street."

I froze, imagining making some mistake and injuring his
back. Rescuing me, Miss Miller calmly motioned me to help her
cover him with the bath blanket, then remove his covers.

We turned him over, removed the cast (which had been cut),
and washed his back—all without mishap. But I was sure glad
that I didn't have to face that patient alone. I was grateful for
Miss Miller's leadership and confidence in my abilities. Instruc-
tors do more than teach technical skills.

Honeymoon in Paraguay

by Clara R. Schmidt

*Clara R. Schmidt lives in Asunción, Paraguay. She spent her
adult life establishing a clinic and hospital working along with
her husband in care of persons with Hansen's disease (leprosy).*

I graduated as a nurse from the Bethel Deaconess Hospital
in Newton, Kansas, on August 20, 1943. Five days later I married Dr. John Schmidt, who had been a doctor to the refugees
in the Chaco of Paraguay for a year and a half. After nine
months in the States, he was taking me back to the work he had
been doing. It was our honeymoon . . . from which we returned after three and a half years with two children!

Even my husband was not prepared for what awaited us.
The hospital had been closed for the nine months since he left;
only the most needed medicines had been given out. The two
former nurses were not continuing. So John and I were alone
with the patients who lined up early the first morning after our
arrival.

We began by taking patient histories. John had me fill them
out in English, though he consulted with them in low German,
which I couldn't understand at the time.

To start work we needed helpers, especially a cook and
someone to do the laundry. Then we invited women from the
villages who were interested in nursing to take a course. Our

first class consisted of seven young women. We quickly learned to work together closely in response to the greatest needs. For instance, when we had surgery scheduled, we taught a class in surgical techniques; when we had a typhoid patient, we taught isolation techniques. To impress upon them the need to protect themselves as well as all of us, we emphasized cleanliness. The students could almost feel the bacilli crawling over them.

These women did things I had never done—whitewashed the unused room of the old hospital, cleaned and sunned beds and bedding, took turns helping in the kitchen and laundry or whatever came along. Soon the hospital was ready for patients. Most had little schooling and we had no textbooks. But one person had attended high school, so her notebooks became the text for the others.

The state of the nursery gave me the greatest shock. Floors were smeared with mud and manure. Cribs were made of rough lumber, with straw sacks as mattresses. Our first baby was premature, born at home and brought to us the next morning. I literally lived and slept with this baby, working hours to get it to nurse, feeding it with a medicine dropper until it did.

The women were used to midwives, so I delivered the babies from the start, consulting with my husband if there were complications. One afternoon while I was helping a nurse with a problem, I noticed my own time had come. Soon my husband had delivered our first son. On the birth certificate John signed as doctor, nurse, and father.

It was cold; instead of putting us in the hospital, John took me home. There we were able to have a warm room to take care of the baby, which John proudly did.

Home to Die

by Marlene Hohne

Marlene Hohne lives in Mindonas, Manitoba. She is a staff nurse in a rural hospital. She has experience in a tuberculosis sanitarium with Eskimos and Indians in northern Canada.

The day staff in the nurses' lounge listened as Colleen gave the night report on the condition of each little patient on the pediatric ward.

When she came to Room 211, she told us Sammie had been brought back from Winnipeg the previous evening by Life Flight (the air ambulance) for "Comfort Care." *That's a good name for looking after the dying,* I reflected. It didn't use words like "terminal" or "death." I guess euphemisms *do* have a place. Besides, Comfort Care reminded us of our duty to relieve distress for the patient, as well as to console and support the family while they tried to cope with the imminent death of their premature infant.

Sammie had been hooked up to a heart monitor all his short life. The doctors in Winnipeg knew there was no cure or hope of survival for this bit of humanity. They thought it would be better for Sammie to be in the hospital near his family.

Sammie had been born seven weeks early to Valerie, a twenty-five-year-old single mother of two other little boys. She had given him his father's last name. But Sammie had been born with several physical abnormalities.

Minutes after his birth, Life Flight was requested to ferry him from our small hospital in northern Manitoba to the neonatal intensive care unit in Winnipeg. There more abnormalities were discovered. Sammie's prognosis was poor.

As we made our rounds, we nurses on the day shift looked in on the tiny infant, now almost six weeks old. He was so small, barely tipping the scales at six pounds. He had a shock of straight, black hair on his oddly shaped head. His black eyes flashed open momentarily, blinking at me as I stood looking at him snuggled against his blue-striped blanket in the oversized crib.

His tongue licked at his lips. It was near feeding time, and he began to cry loudly, as if to tell someone to get him some breakfast. Due to a cleft palate, Sammie needed to be tube fed every four hours. His little feet were clubbed and his little wrists and arms also looked clubbed. The shape of his head was abnormal. Marie, the nurse assigned to his care for the shift, said he was physically handicapped.

When all the children assigned to me were asleep for an after-dinner nap, I returned to Sammie's room. I touched his hand. He pulled my fingers against his tiny, heaving chest to which the heart monitor electrodes were attached. I gently squeezed his tiny crippled hand, and he moved his head slightly, his big black eyes searching for the rest of me. I asked Marie if I could hold him for a while.

"Sure. Go ahead and love him to death."

We looked at each other in shock, then smiled as we both realized it had been a slip of the tongue. Marie walked over to the crib and gently lifted the tiny deformed child and handed him to me.

"Here, Sammie, go to Grandma Liz," Marie said as she laid the child in my hands. Marie touched the soft skin on Sammie's cheek. "Grandma Liz knows how to love a little guy like you," she chuckled at a smile from Sammie. "Yes, baby, Granny here has had a lot of kids! She knows how to love you."

I took the light bundle from Marie and tucked him close to my heart. I saw a tear edge the nurse's eyes.

"Even though you've gone through all that testing and poking, you can still smile, you little puddin'." She patted him lovingly on the back and went to care for another baby.

I laid Sammie back in my hand and talked to him. His clubbed feet lay pulled into a near fetal position, making him look so much smaller than he really was. Sammie's little black eyes darted back and forth, twinkling, as he searched my face and listened to my voice.

As Marie went out of the room, she put a cassette into the tape player and gospel music flooded the room. I cuddled Sammie close, and he snuggled like a soft little kitten.

I sang quietly along with the music, patting his back in time to the music, realizing that all the songs were about heaven.

"Soon you'll be going to heaven, Sammie. I know you're going to like it a lot better than here," I whispered in his tiny ear.

The doctors in the city had sent Sammie to be closer to his parents and family. But his mother, who had come from Winnipeg with the baby in the plane, had stayed at the hospital for only a few minutes after the baby was admitted.

In the five days since then, no one had been in to see him, except this morning when a stout, aging, gray-haired native lady came up to the ward saying she was Sammie's grandmother. Marie told her of his condition as she walked her to Sammie's room. Then she left her alone with her new grandson for the first time.

The old woman stood by the crib watching her grandchild. She seemed afraid to touch the baby. Marie walked back into the room, gently touched the grandmother on the sleeve, and asked if she wanted to hold the baby.

She hesitated, then smiled, showing a mouth empty of teeth,

as she slowly nodded and took off her red jacket. "He's so small!" she whispered as Marie put the child into her arthritic hands.

Marie told her that the baby loved to be held and that he was noticing things now. "Take all the time you want with Sammie; he likes it when you talk to him."

The grandmother sat down on the soft vinyl chair, holding Sammie, sitting forward stiffly. At first she seemed at a loss as to what to say to her kin. "Wee One," she finally ventured, "you are so tiny. I wish I could take you home with me. But, Wee One, I am going to die soon too! Doctor told me last week."

The old woman buried Sammie's face into her neck. "Maybe, just maybe, we'll get to heaven together," she sighed, then continued. "Look for me, Wee One, and I'll look for you."

She traced her gnarled finger over his mouth and Sammie tried to lick it. "Oh, my little Wee One, I love you so." A tear dropped onto the baby's face. "I'm sure your mommy could learn to love you."

Twenty minutes later the grandmother called Marie over and asked her to put the child to bed. "I'll see you soon, Wee One," she whispered in a barely audible voice, "I'll see you soon." Her body quivered with a sob.

Marie took the baby, then laid her hand on the old woman's arm. Marie said the nurses would look after the baby and they would love him. She tucked him into the crib. She asked the grandmother when Sammie's mother would be coming to see the baby.

The old lady shrugged her shoulders. "I don't know," she sighed. "I only know she took the other two kids up north with her boyfriend."

She slowly took her jacket off the chair, awkwardly putting her stiff arms into the sleeves. "I don't know, nurse, I really don't know when she'll come," she whispered as she stared into the little crib.

The old woman shuffled her aching body slowly down the hall to the double doors, her long printed skirt nearly touching her moccasins. Her shoulders were slumped. She wiped her eyes and blew her nose with a tissue.

She opened the door slowly, then stopped, looking back at Marie. "Nurse, tell my Wee One that his old grandma loves him very much, very much." Then she slipped through the big gray door holding it ajar.

I had picked Sammie up from the crib. Now I took him off my chest as the music continued. His big, black eyes found my face and as I talked, a smile curled the edges of his lips.

"Precious Sammie," I murmured. "You are going to live with Jesus soon. And there you will be able to race around heaven and play with a whole bunch of other kids. Your feet will work real good for you then." As I talked softly to him, another smile darted across his narrow face. Then he dropped his head onto my chest, ready to go to sleep while being cuddled.

I sang along with the music, patting and pouring my grand-mother's heart of love into the infant. I kept an eye on the mon-itor as I thought back over the years of the five healthy children I'd raised. Now I was enjoying three beautiful grandchildren. I felt sorry for the mother of this deformed child.

I sat up straight as the monitor hesitated momentarily be-tween 150 and 180. Suddenly it dropped to 123, 111, then 86. Immediately I was on my feet, stimulating Sammie with pats to his back, ready to call Marie. But as I patted him, the monitor jumped its way back up to 166. I breathed a sigh of relief and sat down again.

Sammie tucked his head against my body, then dozed off to sleep, unaware of the activity of the monitor or the pounding of my heart. I thanked God the baby's heartbeat was stable again.

As I held the sleeping baby, I listened to the music but didn't feel like singing now. I thought about the words "Comfort Care" as I rocked Sammie in my arms, but I really wanted this little one to live.

Again, suddenly the monitor dropped to 34, then for a split second it hit 0. The alarm on the monitor gave one quick ting, then quit, edging upward. I was on my feet again, patting the child's back. I couldn't see Marie anywhere, but I called her name as I stimulated this little life that was fading in my arms. Marie wasn't around. Slowly, the numbers on the monitor eased their way back up to the regular beat.

I held Sammie for another half hour. He was asleep and breathing heavily. I laid him down on his tummy in the big hospital crib. After straightening the little limbs the best I could, I tucked the blue baby blanket around him.

"Sleep, little Sammie, Jesus will come for you soon." I looked at the empty chair on which his mother could be sitting. Maybe she's afraid of death, I thought.

I left the ward with mixed emotions at the end of my shift. As I passed Sammie's room for the last time I saw the monitor once again fluctuate to the lesser numbers as the new shift of nurses took over the care of the child into whom I had been allowed to pour a bit of love, if only for a few moments.

Foo-Fooing

by Anne Warkentin Dyck

Anne Warkentin Dyck lives in Swift Current, Saskatchewan. She worked in Indonesia for twenty years with Mennonite Central Committee. Her focus was on midwifery, giving care in clinics, and operating room nursing. Since then she has worked in a senior citizen's home and chronic care hospital. She volunteers time with a Alzheimer's disease support group.

When you work in another culture, how do you respect traditions while trying to change things which may create health hazards? Which practices are truly dangerous? Which are harmless even though they seem unusual to us? The answers may vary, but I believe the bottom line is *compassion*.

The time it was hardest for me to live this out was when I allowed a patient to *foo-foo* right in the hospital, much to the dismay and surprise of some of our nursing staff. I even surprised myself!

The incident happened while I was on assignment in Indonesia. In addition to my nursing responsibilities, I went as a midwife to villagers' homes in Halmahera, an isolated, northern island. One local custom, practiced mainly among the most rural village people, was that after delivery the new mother needed to foo-foo. There's no adequate English word for this practice. It is the same Indonesian word used for smoking co-

conuts on a rack over a glowing fire to shrink and preserve them for export.

After a home delivery, family members or friends would put a glowing coconut husk under the new mother's bed, right beneath her uterus area. This was supposed to help the mother pass "dirty blood" left in the uterus. They considered it especially important if there was a lump in the mother's lower abdomen (the very thing which encouraged me, because then I knew the uterus was contracted and she wouldn't hemorrhage).

Though I did not accept foo-fooing as having medicinal value, I usually looked the other way when families did this in their own homes. Sometimes they quietly brought the fire in while I was still there. Other times they waited until I left.

When my permission was formally asked, I never refused, but usually pointed out two things. First, it was not necessary because the lump in the mother's lower abdomen was a good sign. Second, if they did bring the foo-foo in, they needed to keep a close watch on the little barefoot children who invariably came running up to mother's bed. Sometimes we'd end up with additional patients when youngsters burned their toes because they came too close to the foo-foo fire.

I was able to live with this custom as long as it was practiced in people's own homes. But my tolerance was tested at the hospital.

Many times the doctor had to look after medical needs on another part of the island, leaving me in charge. He was the only doctor in the only hospital on an island of 50,000 people.

Once while the doctor was gone, a woman was brought in who was experiencing a difficult labor. Her trip had taken four to five hours by sailboat. Her genitalia were swollen and bruised from some of the local *dukuns*' (medicine man or woman) treatment. Her bladder was *very* full. Worst of all, she had a high fever and chills, which I diagnosed as malaria and vaginal infection.

After catheterization, when the bladder was empty, the birth wasn't as difficult as I had feared. But the woman remained dangerously ill. I confess to feeling disgusted and impatient when, a few hours later, a message came from the hospital that her husband was preparing to take her home. If that happened I doubted the woman would live. If she stayed, I felt she still had a chance.

In trying to reason with the husband, I soon sensed there was something he was uneasy about and didn't want to tell me. Then it dawned on me. I asked him directly, "Are you taking her home because you have to foo-foo?"

Obviously uncomfortable, he slowly admitted this was so. My impatience and annoyance left me as I saw this man in turmoil, torn between his tradition and wanting good medical help for his wife. I had told him, after delivery, that we would try hard to save his wife, but in her condition I could not give him real assurance that she would live.

"If she dies," he explained, "her mother and grandmother would never forgive me if I hadn't even tried to foo-foo. We'll never know whether she might have lived if I had foo-fooed."

He didn't put any pressure on me to let him do it there because he was aware that hospitals don't do that sort of thing. Or do they? Well, *I* allowed it. You can imagine the amazement among our hospital staff when I asked them to see about getting a glowing coconut husk from the kitchen. (All our cooking fuel was coconut husks, so that was no problem.)

The husband readily agreed that if he could "foo-foo," he would make no further attempt to discharge his wife until we felt ready to go. As I expected, he was true to his word. Whether because of the foo-foo, or in spite of it, the woman recovered. I believe a life was saved because I opted for compassion and caring and thus enabled her to stay to finish treatment. To God be the glory!

Say What You Mean

by Florence Nafziger

Florence Nafziger lives in Goshen, Indiana. She spent forty years in India teaching nursing for Mennonite Board of Missions.

My first real job after passing the State Boards in Colorado, was as head nurse at St. Luke's Hospital in Boise, Idaho. The change was dramatic and a little traumatic. From the sheltered environment of a Mennonite community I went to an Episcopal environment where we spent morning chapel mostly on our knees repeating a daily litany of prayers. The administrator and the nursing superintendent were from New England and spoke with a clipped British accent quite different from what I was used to.

The nursing environment was also different. Things I thought were nursing history were still being done at St. Luke's, such as the way our shifts were scheduled.

I found it difficult to plan the duty schedule for the student nurses on my ward so that they had three hours off plus an hour for two meals. Being the head nurse, I was expected to assign duties to the student nurses according to their experience—yet I had to depend on them to get the work of the unit done.

I was just learning to cope when a class of probationers was admitted. When some were assigned to my ward, I learned a lesson that would influence my subsequent career as a nursing educator in India.

The eager "probies," who had to be tested for three months before receiving their caps, also worked on the wards for several hours each day. To my astonishment, their teachers did not come with them to supervise them. *I* was expected to do this in addition to attending to the patients on my ward.

One afternoon a physician's order came through to get an X-ray taken of one of our male patients. The X-ray lab was down a flight of stairs in the basement, so I told a "probie" to take the patient down in a wheelchair. She hurried off but soon came back to ask breathlessly, "How do I get him down?"

I glanced at the elevator opposite my desk. Exasperated at what I thought was a silly question, I said, "Why, take him down the stairs." I hoped my flippancy would bring her to her senses. Then I sat down at my desk to continue some charting.

Soon I heard an ominous thumping. My blood ran cold as I pictured the "probie" pushing the wheelchair down the three steps to the first landing. I held my breath, anticipating a bumpity-bump, then a scream as she sent the hapless patient down the remaining flight of steps on his own!

I waited. But there was only silence.

Then Miss Smith, our formidable nursing superintendent, was standing at my desk. I hastily stood.

"Miss Nafziger," she said in her clipped New England speech, "I just met one of your students pushing a patient's wheelchair down the stairs."

I stared.

"She seems to think you told her to do it," she explained.

I looked down at my charts, then across the hall at the elevator. "Well I *did*, but I didn't expect her to do it."

"Miss Nafziger, remember this: don't ever tell a student to do something that you don't expect her to do." But before she marched away, I'm sure I saw a twinkle in her eye.

I needed that warning. It kept me from saying many foolish things during my subsequent career in India teaching nursing.

The Night the Angels Sang

by Glenda Hartzler

Glenda Hartzler lives in Belleville, Pennsylvania. This story occurred more than ten years ago and the experience is still clear in her memory. She has worked twenty years in nursing, mostly in critical care and some administration. She also teaches vocational students in an extended care setting.

Several years ago I was working as a staff nurse in the intensive coronary care unit of our local hospital. The three-to-eleven nurse finished her report and the other nurses and I started making our rounds. We had a ten-bed unit, and each of us took care of different aspects of a patient's needs.

We had finished checking nine patients and were ready to care for Charlie, who was terminally ill. Because he and his family had decided against heroics or life support, he had no monitor attached. I do not know whether Charlie was a Christian, but I remember him as a kind and gentle man, always appreciative of any kindness. We did what we could for him and left. Everything had seemed normal, given his condition.

But later, back at the desk finishing some charting, I heard beautiful music. Initially I thought the stereo was on. "We certainly have a good station to listen to tonight," I said.

My co-workers looked at me like I was crazy. "What are you

talking about, Glenda? We don't hear anything."

But the music continued. No words, just the most beautiful music I had ever heard. Finally I said half jokingly, "I think the angels came for Charlie. Let's go check!"

We went to Charlie's room, not knowing what to expect since he was not on the monitor. He was taking his last breath.

I can't explain the music except to say that I felt we were standing on holy ground and there were angels around.

I will never forget Charlie.

The Two-Faced Man

by Naomi Weaver

Naomi Weaver lives in Nazareth, Israel. She has done staff nursing and nursing education in the U.S., Zambia, Tanzania, Zimbabwe, Kenya, Haiti, and Israel.

The circle of staff members gathered for prayer in the African hospital was broken when an urgent call came for the doctors. Responding to the call they found a patient whom we would for weeks thereafter refer to as "the two-faced man."

It turned out the man had literally had his face halved by the *panga* (knife) of a drunken brawler. This included a slash through the brain. Making things worse, the well-intentioned but frightened relatives had tipped the homemade stretcher too far and the patient had slid to the ground.

The surgeon had limited equipment and nothing more than the facilities of a mission hospital in the African bush. Almost despairing before he began, he cleaned the wounds, wired the jaws and, during the extensive repairs of the head wound, found that probably some brain tissue had been lost. The man survived the initial cleanup and was placed in the male ward of the hospital. Would he live until morning?

I came on the scene the second morning following the accident. I found, as I assisted a student nurse to care for the man, not a comatose and paralyzed patient as I had expected, but a wakeful patient trying to tell us his needs. Because his jaws were wired shut, he was forced to communicate with his eyes, hand signals, and what garbled sounds he could make. I got the message that he wanted paper and pencil.

In English he wrote, "I'm hungry, can I have some tea?"

He had no problems as he sipped the tea from a straw placed through the space where teeth were missing.

Weeks later this man—no longer two-faced and with full mental faculties, walked from the hospital with the aid of only a cane, thanking the little god (doctor) who had saved his life. Was it pluck or prayer that pulled this man through the amazing ordeal? Perhaps God planned to use this man to speak to others about the one who takes the broken pieces and not only mends them, but makes a beautiful whole.

It's Not Over Until It's Over

by Naomi Weaver

*Naomi Weaver lives in Nazareth, Israel. She has done staff
nursing and nursing education in the U.S., Zambia, Tanzania,
Zimbabwe, Kenya, Haiti, and Israel.*

Several years ago while serving in a small hospital in the East
African bush, I was told that the doctor would be gone all day.
He was also taking the only car. We hoped and prayed that no
patient transfer should become necessary.

But about noon I was called to the "emergency room" to see
a man with a slash in his chest wall. He was conscious and stable, so I proceeded to gingerly remove bandages. The rising
blood pressure and removal of bandages caused fresh bleeding. This made it difficult to determine the layers that needed
stitching.

I asked another nurse for help, but it was obvious the patient
urgently needed to go to a hospital with a doctor. We managed
to give a typed and cross-matched unit of blood while searching for a car and driver. Happily, the pastor of the adjoining
church was home and agreed to take the patient in his car.

As he drove down the road with patient and family in the
backseat of his car, he heard a gasp and turned to see a non-
breathing patient. As is the custom in East Africa, the family be-

gan to wail. Nothing could persuade the family to continue what they believed to be a futile trip to the hospital, so the pastor turned the car around to head home.

Several miles into the return journey, activity and noise from the backseat attracted the pastor's attention again. A glance in the rearview mirror showed the patient to be sitting up and breathing normally!

Being There

by Anna Frances Wenger

Anna Frances Wenger lives in Stone Mountain, Georgia. Her first job was a staff nurse in Cleveland, Ohio, on a medical surgical unit as a night nurse. She worked in nursing education for thirty years including such settings as Ghana, Haiti, Nicaragua, and Germany. Transcultural nursing is her strong interest.

I was the only nurse on the night shift with twenty-five clients on a medical/surgical floor. As I was busy getting medications set up, taking vital signs, and checking on new post-op patients, Edna's light went on. She was a cancer patient, about forty-six, and couldn't sleep. She asked me to talk.

I went to her side and touched her hand. I don't remember what we talked about or how long, but I do remember the room was dark; light from the hall filtered in. As I listened my mind drifted to all my tasks and I impulsively turned my watch—ever so slightly—to see the time.

She said, "Must you go? You don't have time?"

"Oh yes, it's okay, I'm here," I replied. But until then I had not been really *present* with her. She had asked for only a few minutes of quality time. I thought she wouldn't see in the dark, but she sensed my partial attention.

That was more than thirty-five years ago. That incident taught me about the human ability to sense response (or lack of it) from others. I learned to respect the mystery of personal interaction and the therapeutic value of caring through presence. Edna and I had had a nurse/patient relationship that was good for both of us. Through this experience I grew in my ability to respond to her—and to others, both professionally and personally.

My Most Frightening Nursing Experience

by Bonita Driver

Bonita Driver lives in Goshen, Indiana. She worked in Puerto Rico in a rural hospital and clinic. For thirty-eight years she served with Mennonite Board of Missions in Spain, Uruguay, Argentina, and Bolivia doing hospital work and informal nursing in the community.

More than thirty years ago, my husband, John, and I were assigned to work in a remote rural area in Puerto Rico, far from the nearest town with any medical services. A small frame structure was built to offer medical and dental services on a weekly basis.

The Mennonite hospital, located in La Plata, sent the doctor and the dentist to serve the community through our little "clinic." My job was to be the nurse. This service was much appreciated, since transportation to the nearest towns was sometimes difficult and health care insurance was almost unknown.

One day a middle-aged woman came for medical attention at one of the weekly clinics. I do not recall what the medical diagnosis was, but I do remember giving her the injection of antibiotics the doctor had ordered.

During the following week the woman sent word that she needed another shot. She asked if I could come to her house and give it to her. I checked her clinic record, gathered my equipment, and asked my husband to accompany me down the winding mountain road to her house.

She insisted the first injection had helped her so much that she should get a second ampule. Since she was so insistent, I checked her further and administered the antibiotic into her hip.

To my horror, she stood up beside the bed, gasping for breath. She flung open the rough wooden shutters on the window, saying she could barely breathe. When she involuntarily urinated, I realized she was experiencing a strong allergic reaction.

I was not prepared for such a crisis. I had no ephedrine with me to open her bronchial passages and insure her ability to continue breathing. I helped her back onto the bed.

Then, because I was so frightened, I dashed out into the adjacent room where John was conversing with the woman's husband and asked John to come in quickly. We both placed our hands on the woman and prayed for God's merciful intervention.

By the time we finished the prayer, her appearance had changed notably. She took several deep breaths and her pulse became strong once more. She got up from the bed and thanked us for the shot.

Soon, thanking God, we left.

But you can be sure that before we left, I impressed upon the woman the seriousness of what had just happened. I warned her never again to ask for any antibiotics until she had been thoroughly tested for possible reactions.

Midwifery in Puerto Rico

by Rachel Shiffler Holderread

Rachel Shiffler Holderread lives in Corvallis, Oregon. She worked as a midwife in Puerto Rico for six years. She also worked as a staff nurse in labor and birth as well as in home care for disturbed teenagers in the Pacific Northwest.

At 1:15 one morning in 1959, my husband and I were suddenly awakened by a loud knock on the front door. It always takes a moment to realize that there is no time to waste. This might be one of those families where the birth comes quickly. We rushed to the door with one eye still half asleep.

An excited man greeted us. "*Buenos noches.* My wife has the pains all night and most of yesterday. Can you come right away? Her time has come."

I stepped into my uniform and grabbed my two bags. Meanwhile, my husband unlocked the car, checked that all four tires were inflated, that there was gas in the tank, and that the electric lantern was working.

While I gathered my final things, my husband asked the man, "Do you have electricity? Can you drive back in, close to your house? Is it muddy?"

In a few minutes my husband closed the car door and waved to me and the eager father as we drove off down the road.

After driving as far as we could, the man suggested that we leave the car and walk the rest of the way, "*un poso lejos* (a little far)."

That was fine, but after a while, I finally asked, "Where is the house?"

"You can't see it from here. We go down this valley and up that little mountain," he answered.

Sure enough! I spied a faint light in a small shack and asked, "This is it?"

"Oh no, that is where my mother-in-law lives. We are more farther."

I peered ahead into the darkness every time we came over a small rise or around a corner in the trail. Somewhere ahead there had to be another light seeping through a window or the cracks in this man's house.

Finally he said, "See over there? That is it."

Indeed, over and around two more rugged mountains I could see a small twinkle! *Oh no,* I thought to myself, *I can't go another step.* I was exhausted! But self-pity gets one nowhere, and knowing that the end of the trail was near helped me muster up new courage. Before long we were there.

The house was propped up on one side by the mountain and on the other with stilts. There were no steps; we had to climb up a couple of feet to get in the door.

Breathlessly I headed for the only bedroom in the house. There I found an expectant mother calmly walking around. Between breaths I asked if she was having hard pains.

"Oh no, very simple," she replied. I wondered who was suffering all those "pains" the father told us about. After further questions, I suggested that I prepare her for delivery just in case things started and ended in a hurry.

In the small room there were two more beds closely fitted together, with six small children foot to foot in one and five larger youngsters in the other. These rural people loved excitement, no matter what the cause. One by one the neighbors had arrived. I counted five men and seven women, with only a scant curtain between them and the "delivery room."

My seven helpers and observers, concerned that my every need be fulfilled, were busily lighting candles, since there was no electricity. But one special candle was hid under a small table, supposedly out of my sight. This was to direct God's and the virgin Mary's eyes to this suffering woman. At times I saw figures kneeling in front of the candle saying their rosary.

I proceeded to the kitchen to see if water had been heated. Yes, there in a small dipperlike container was about one pint of water. I looked around and found a gallon fruit can. Filling and heating it for future use, I carefully placed it on the flat cement charcoal stove, which was about three feet square. There was no chimney in the house; the smoke escaped through the holes and cracks in the walls and ceiling.

At the proper time I gave the mother medication. Her blood pressure was normal, the fetal heart tones strong and regular. Everything seemed fine.

The only complication was that I had been called five hours too early! Of course I waited. One never knows what might happen. Besides, I didn't want to be called back again to walk over those trails if I didn't have to.

I made use of my wait. It was a good time to hand out tracts and gospels and practice my Spanish. In the course of the conversation one lady told me that she knew about me. I had delivered her husband's other wife's child. I tried to find out more diplomatically, but the explanation was confusing.

Soon the mother's pains began increasing. Her godmother asked if she could give her some tea made of grapefruit leaves.

"It will give her much *animo*." I approved.

Finally, the beginning of the end was near. The final preparations were made, with everything kept as sterile as possible—under the circumstances. Mosquitoes, *mimis* (a little bit-ing fly), and moths offered a lot of competition.

"Close your mouth. Bear down until I tell you to breathe." Presto! A fine big boy—number twelve for this experienced mother—was born at 6:05 a.m.

Once the mother was completely cared for, everyone gathered around the small living room table to watch the bathing of this miracle. By then all the children were up and excited about "this-year's baby."

The father carefully looked him over and said, "He looks just like me." Then he added, "I now have six boys and six girls. We will call him a Bible name. How about Moses?"

It was final. Moses was dressed in a yellow dress since that color was thought to bring him good luck throughout his life.

When we were finished, three men walked out to the road with me, carrying my things. They checked the tires for me—you can never tell how long tires will last on such rough roads—and directed me in turning around in the narrow place. They even offered to accompany me home in case there were any problems.

I assured them that everything would be fine. I have gone out alone on many calls, and I thoroughly trusted the mountain people of Puerto Rico.

With exchanged *gracias*, I headed for home. Tired? Yes, but singing within, thanking God.

Village Health Care and the Mother-in-Law

by Katherine E. Yutzy

Katherine E. Yutzy lives in Goshen, Indiana. She spent seven and a half years in India with the Mennonite Board of Missions. She has worked with migratory families and in community health, nursing administration, and nursing education.

While I worked in India as a nursing educator, one of my tasks was to begin a health care program in some of the villages close to our hospital.

One of the first villages to which I took my students was typical in that the people were not sure whether to trust me or not. I was a foreigner. Their village had managed to survive for centuries without interference from foreign ladies. What could we do for them now?

We met with the village chief, then with the council. How could they refuse? I thought. It did not cost them anything, yet they could get their needed immunizations and physical examinations. Otherwise they'd have to travel to the hospital for out-patient care.

Not only was there reluctance from the villagers, some of the medical and nursing staff of the hospital also did not think the village-based health care program was a good idea. For one thing, it would take patients away from the hospital, and the hospital needed patients to survive.

We finally agreed that we would try it for one six-month period and see how it worked. Then the program would be evaluated both for educational value as well as for any decrease in hospital patient load.

Assessment was the first task. We went from house to house to find out who lived where, what the makeup of each family was, and what medical problems existed. We treated whatever we could as we went—often skin lesions or scabies. Many patients were referred to the outpatient department of the hospital for such things as intestinal parasites, anemia, and other conditions for which we did not have standing orders.

I had midwifery students with me, so we did prenatal care as well as checking all postpartum (after delivery) mothers and newborn infants. We did such things as hemoglobin checks, height and weight, urinalysis, and fetal heart checks. Each person or family referred to the hospital was given a card saying that the community health nurses had made the referral and indicating the reasons. These people did not have to wait in long lines but could register much more quickly.

We continued to go from house to house until we had contacted all the homes. Since these were mostly farming families, we needed to make our calls while they were in the home. This was usually at lunchtime, the first hour after lunch, or later in the evening. The villages were close enough so the students and I could walk and carry our bags of equipment.

One morning we had finished the assessment in the initial village and were checking a postpartum mother and her new baby. Just then a woman asked us to come to the other side of the village and see her pregnant daughter-in-law. We made that our second stop. This is what happened.

Shushi was the wife of the youngest son. As the newest daughter-in-law, it was her task to do much of the housework and cooking. She also was the last to eat because it was her responsibility to serve all the others.

Shushi was nearly seven months into her first pregnancy. For the past couple weeks she had little or no fetal movement, and none at all for the last week. The mother-in-law was worried. Since the home remedies had not helped, she called us.

After much discussion, she invited us into the home. We did a prenatal check for Shushi with the mother-in-law at our elbows. We did hear faint fetal heart sounds. Shushi was quite anemic, with a hemoglobin of less than four milligram/percent. Normal hemoglobin for healthy women is twelve to sixteen grams per one hundred milliliters of blood. She was pale, her conjunctiva was nearly white, and she said she was very tired all the time. There did not seem to be any other problem.

We did not have treatment with us, so she was referred to the outpatient department of the hospital. We had told her that at the hospital she might be given further blood tests or even need to stay in the hospital for a night or more.

The family accompanied her to the hospital and all seemed well. She was given iron medication. Along with this she was told she had to have a balanced diet every day if the infant was to survive. The mother-in-law agreed to the treatment. Even some of the housework was shared by other household members.

Soon the fetal movements were back to normal and Sushi's hemoglobin made a steady climb toward the norm.

In the meantime, we always checked on Shushi when we visited the village. Her color improved, as did her energy level. Finally the day arrived when we visited the village and were told that Shushi had given birth to a healthy male. We were to come see them both. We never saw a more grateful mother-in-law or family.

This was "our" son, we were told. It was "God's will that he is living and well," the family declared. It was a wonderful opportunity for testimony and a happy ending to a potentially dangerous situation.

Shushi's mother-in-law became an advocate for all the pregnant women in the village. She made sure each one was seen by the nurses and sent to the hospital if referred. Later, when we had floods in the north and cholera inoculations were to be given to everyone who traveled, she encouraged others to become a part of the program.

We also gave all the routine immunizations for children. I don't remember a time when we set up a "clinic"—which consisted of a table under the tree or in front of someone's house—that Shushi's mother-in-law did not come to visit with us. Yes, the foreigner and her students could be helpful and were welcome in this village and other surrounding ones.

When the six months and the evaluation of the village health care program were completed, we found we had *increased* the patient load at the hospital through our referrals to the outpatient department. Some outpatients needed to be admitted for further treatment. The pleased doctors and nurses gave us their support to continue village health care as partners in providing adequate health care in India.

Taking Risks

by Ruth Hartzler Martin

*Ruth Hartzler Martin lives in Lancaster, Pennsylvania. She
served in Indonesia with Mennonite Central Committee. She
has been in nursing administration in acute care and
psychiatric hospitals.*

Chang was ill with tetanus. We suspected that his tetanus
had been acquired through the large sacral decubiti (bedsores)
he had had for some time. Chang's bedsores were the result of
immobility, probably brought about by congenital syphilis. His
legs were paralyzed and severely contracted so that he could
not walk. He had to lie on his back with his knees propped up
with pillows, or lie on his side.

Chang was Chinese. In north central Java, Chinese are a mi-
nority of the population but have traditionally been wealthy because of their involvement in business and retail sales. However, apparently Chang's family—which was attentive and
came to visit him—weren't so wealthy since he was in the
hospital's second class (though not third class) accommoda-
tions.

I worked in that small hospital in Taju, Java, as a nurse with
the Mennonite Central Committee in the early 1960s. I recall no
history of any rehabilitation efforts that might have been at-

tempted. It is quite possible that traditional, fatalistic attitudes overshadowed any thoughts of rehabilitation. Certainly any successful rehabilitation looked like a long, tedious, and expensive process.

Chang was alert and aware of events in his immediate environment. He had been transferred to us from a nursing home so we could treat his tetanus. His recovery from tetanus was going smoothly, and he had progressed from intravenous therapy to taking oral liquids. Maintenance of fluid and electrolyte balance was the primary treatment focus. Other possible treatments were not available.

Intravenous fluids were scarce and used carefully in any treatment. Sometimes we could purchase them from a supplier who lived two or three hours away by car. Other times the supplier had none and we had to make our own—a task for which we could barely meet minimum standards. So we were always glad when patients could take fluids orally to maintain their own fluid balance. (At that time we didn't have IV antibiotics and the many other medications now given intravenously.)

One Sunday the hospital's doctor and I agreed that I would make rounds at the hospital that afternoon. We were aware of no major problems. Although I regularly worked in the outpatient clinics rather than the hospital, making rounds with the physician was not unusual. So I was comfortable making rounds for him. I rode my bicycle the mile or so from home to the hospital that warm, tropical afternoon.

During rounds I learned that Chang's oral intake had decreased below the necessary level. The nursing staff had not gained his cooperation in increasing it. In the tropical heat this situation cannot be allowed to go on long. I phoned the doctor, and we decided to insert a nasogastric tube. It would be easier to give liquids that way than to restart the IV.

As I prepared the materials to insert the tube, Chang pleaded with me not to insert the tube. I explained his need for fluids, then proceeded to insert it. I had inserted N-G tubes many times and was comfortable with my ability to do it properly.

Suddenly, during the insertion, he was still and unresponsive. He wasn't breathing. There was no pulse. We didn't know about CPR at that time, so there was nothing else to do but accept his death.

But the questions flooded in. What had happened? Why? Should I have listened to his pleading not to insert the N-G tube? Would he have taken more fluids orally if he had been given a choice between the tube and oral fluids? Did he have some premonition of the tube's lethal effect on him?

How did his family feel about me? And the other staff who were assisting me—did they blame me for causing his death? Did everyone know that I was really trying to help him when this happened? How would I live with the knowledge that I contributed so directly to Chang's death? Could I forgive myself? Was Chang ready to meet God?

Our doctor was understanding, and I felt his support. He never conveyed any questions about my competence to safely insert N-G tubes. None of the staff conveyed a diminished confidence in me, either.

I have also sought and felt God's love and understanding through this event. I trust God to be fair to Chang. When I think of him and that event, I feel sad and humble, but not guilty. I was acting on Chang's behalf, and I trust God to understand and forgive. I have felt that understanding and forgiveness. This event has not inhibited me from taking risks to provide caring help to others.

The Cow's Tail

by Lena Graber

Lena Graber lives in Goshen, Indiana. She spent twelve years in Nepal and ten years in India serving with Mennonite Board of Missions. She started a school of nursing in both countries.

I was a nurse in Nepal for many years, where it was common for people to come to the hospital when they were ill. But if they learned they were going to die, they often went home to their family, tribe, or village when nothing more could be done. Many Hindus had rituals that they tried to do as they were dying—for example, some wanted to die with their feet in a certain river.

One time we had a gentleman who did not want to leave the hospital when he knew he was going to die. However, he wanted to die holding onto a cow's tail. The family brought the cow to the hospital, but the man was on the second floor, so there wasn't any way to get the cow to the patient. The staff wanted to be sensitive to his needs. Since holding the tail seemed important, we had a conference to figure out the best way to help him.

We came up with a plan and approached the family and the patient. Yes, indeed, it was an agreeable plan! We stationed the cow outside the hospital with a rope tied to its tail. Then the rope was fed up through the second floor window into the

room and over to the bed of the dying man. He grasped the
rope tied to the cow's tail.

He died holding that rope.

Night Ride

by Marianne Schlegal

Marianne Schlegal lives in New Hamburg, Ontario. She has worked on Indian reservations in Canada where she was the only health professional available. She has served in Botswana and the U.S. in home health care and gerontology.

The short winter days in Alberta's north are mainly sunny and cold, except for a chinook wind now and then blowing over the Rockies. Nights are long and crispy cold. I was often the community nurse on call at Calling Lake during the mid-sixties.

Many nights after I tucked myself in bed for the night, a car would come up the road. I would hear a strong fast knock on the door below. Sometimes parents would bring a feverish, crying child or request a visit. Sometimes a mother needed assistance with labor and delivery, or an accident had occurred, or some other emergency couldn't wait until daybreak.

One night began with a middle-aged man having severe chest pain. Following some questions, examination, and Demerol pain medication, we decided to take him to Athabasca Hospital, which was some forty-five miles south over a bumpy, snowy road.

Inez, the kindergarten teacher, drove the VW as I kept watch over my patient. For a while the man had no perceptible pulse rate, but his condition improved before we arrived at the hospital around midnight. He was admitted with the diagnosis of a severe heart attack.

Inez and I, tired and hungry, were invited to have sandwiches and hot coffee in the hospital kitchen. Once we were warm and nourished by the northern hospitality we headed home, thanking God that all had gone well. The patient was alive and in good hands.

On reaching our home community, we met a man with a dog team sledding toward us. Recognizing the nurse's car, he waved his hands furiously. When we stopped, he communicated, in broken English and Cree, something about a baby. I knew his wife was almost due, so we headed for the small one-room house only a mile down the road. They had lost two babies previously.

After examining the mother, I decided we needed to take her and return to the hospital again. Looking at Inez, I asked if she was willing to be my driver—just in case the baby would not wait. Then I grabbed towels and blankets from the clinic, and we headed out into the night.

The hospital staff was surprised to see us back so soon. Our mother gave birth to a healthy little girl while we got warmed by our second lunch of the night in Athabasca Hospital.

"Yes, your man had a severe coronary," the nurses said. "He'll be here for some time."

Going home was a good feeling, a time of thankfulness and praise to God that all went well. The sun was dawning on a new day—a day of challenge and maybe some rest.

Several weeks later I described this night to my mother. That was the night she had awakened and felt the need to pray for me, she informed me.

Appalachian Nurse

by Beulah Nice

Beulah Nice lives in Morrison, Illinois. She served for twenty years on the faculty of Mennonite College of Nursing of Bloomingtonn, Illinois. She has worked as a staff nurse in Colorado, Illinois, and Ohio.

It was a lovely morning. I chose to accompany my student nurse and the regional staff nurse with whom she worked in the Pine Mountain and Wallins districts in southeastern Kentucky. I was the instructor from the Mennonite hospital in Bloomington, Illinois, for this extension program in rural Appalachia in the late 1960s.

I helped gather supplies for the day and noted which McBee cards we were taking with us. (The cards gave background information on each patient as well as a list of specific checks and types of nursing care to be performed.) I noted the knowledgeable way my young student checked her nursing bag. Then we were on our way to the parking lot. Bronco No. 1044 was ours for the day. This sturdy, Jeep-like vehicle was able to go up, down, and around some rough, scenic trails!

After inching through Harlan's crowded traffic, we merrily rolled past little houses along the banks of a stream. Then we passed a rough dwelling, the gathering place of a group of worshipers who reputedly handled snakes to test their faith. We climbed around, up, and over Pine Mountain until we had a glorious view marred only by the rough scars of strip mines on the distant mountainside.

Descending from the mountain, we continued through an interesting little valley until we reached Martha's place. The shack was humble but clean. Martha had diabetes and hypertension. She was too heavy, and needed instruction on dietary habits. She didn't want to give up her diet of beans cooked with fatback, corn bread, biscuits, and gravy—but she listened and indicated that she understood.

Chances were that she would continue to do as she pleased until the next visit of the nurses! Oh, well, how different was she than many others back in Bloomington?

Back in the Bronco, we backtracked five miles over our earlier trail to a new trailer next to a mountain stream. Sally, our patient, greeted us at the door in her birthday suit!

She had been discharged from the hospital the previous week after receiving treatment for burns on her back, buttocks, and thighs, suffered when her nylon nightgown caught fire. The story was that she not only smoked heavily but was also a drug user. And it was far more comfortable to walk around without the irritation of clothes when her scars were still so sensitive.

I visited with the husband while the student and staff nurses gave Sally her therapeutic bath in the tub. A cup of coffee was generously offered, and I accepted. Soon Sally's brother appeared and wanted to speak to the nurses. He ran the little grocery store up the road and controlled Sally's medicine, since she couldn't and her husband had been partially paralyzed by a stroke. Today the brother asked whether he should get a refill of her pain prescription—he thought she was using it too heavily. But Sally screamed at him that he just wanted to see her suffer! It took diplomacy to satisfy both sides.

By then it was eleven o'clock. We needed to drive back over

the mountain and wind our way fifteen miles farther down another valley. Along the way we stopped at a little cafeteria to order hamburgers and coffee. Oh, those hamburgers—and that delicious mountain air! As we left, the student drove the Bronco and did well, down-shifting easily on a sharp turn as we came up behind a loaded coal truck grinding up the mountain. As we headed down the other side, I secretly wished she would take the curves a bit more slowly!

Next we visited Flora in another beautiful valley. The scenery was delightful. We had to ford a stream, cross a railroad track, then wind around another hillside to reach a more prosperous-appearing place. The homes were neater but not pretentious.

Flora greeted me with a hug. "Of course I remember you!" she cried.

At age seventy-five, Flora had diabetes and hypertension, and had lost one leg. She said she was too sick to cooperate when it was amputated, but if she had been aware of what it was like to be without a leg, she never would have consented—she would rather have died!

I could see that a special relationship was developing between Flora and my student nurse. The staff nurse had previously suggested special dietary teaching was needed, so the student worked at it. I proudly watched her explain a chart made with pictures and various symbols to indicate the time of day, such as a crowing rooster for breakfast time.

Flora couldn't read, but did understand the symbols, and her eyes lit up as comprehension dawned. Phil, Flora's handsome and devoted husband—at least her second and younger than she—came in to listen to us. After making sure she understood how to take her pills, we left.

Turning off the main road, we scrambled over a muddy rut, chose the proper fork, and negotiated the slippery hillside which ended up in Joe's yard among the scratching chickens.

Stepping over the trickle of dishwater which was usually

tossed over the porch railing, and admiring the mountain view, we went up the rickety steps, knocked, and entered a reasonably clean kitchen. In the next room we found Joe and his wife, as well as a daughter-in-law and granddaughter. The latter were "temporarily" residing there. All were eager to visit, including the little girl, who was dreadfully spoiled by Joe.

This sixty-year-old man had black lung as a result of being a coal miner for many years. He was so short of breath that he wondered if he would ever again be able to get enough air. A positive pressure outfit (a piece of equipment for people with respiratory problems) sat in the bedroom. Joe had been using it for several days, but we again went over the directions and had him show us how to manipulate the controls and add the medication. He understood.

Then we checked his blood pressure, listened to his querulous wife, and asked how well he was sticking to his diet. Not too well, we surmised. Further teaching was in order.

Finally we headed back down the mountain and over the trail to the highway. Back in the office there was charting to do, as well as checking messages and supplies. A problem came up that required the help of the social worker. Consulting with the physical therapist about another patient's needs also took time.

There was a referral in the basket for a new patient in the Pine Mountain area. Good! Tomorrow the student would have a chance to do the initial workup. She seemed well oriented and made good contact with the friendly yet proud mountain people. I had no fears that she would overstep the bounds of common courtesy.

Each day was different and offered opportunities for different aspects of nursing. I said, "See you tomorrow!" and left with the feeling that we had made a small contribution to these appreciative people.

Cancer Didn't Stop Her

by Gwan Hsiu-man

Gwan Hsiu-man lives in Hualien, Taiwan. She has been the head nurse of obstetrics and gynecology for several years at Mennonite Christian Hospital. For more than thirty-five years she served in Taiwan with the General Conference Commission on Overseas Mission teaching nursing and community health, and establishing mountain clinics. Helen Willms translated her story.

In 1977 while I was getting my practical education at Chang-hua Christian Hospital in Taiwan, I discovered one day a painful area on my left chest wall. X-rays revealed white spots on the sixth rib. The biopsy report said it was a fibrous tumor.

My strength rapidly decreased. A week later I was bleeding into my chest cavity and had trouble breathing. I was then transferred to the Veterans Hospital in Taipei. There they surgically removed the sixth rib, finding I had an infiltration of fibrous malignant cells called fibrous histiocytoma.

The doctor said the tumor was vascular and surrounded by many nerve fibers. It was difficult to remove and caused much bleeding. Two months later I had to have surgery again, for which they prepared 7,000 cc's (over seven quarts) of blood.

Still they weren't able to get the whole tumor, and so I had to undergo radiation therapy. My condition had become serious. I felt awful.

When I graduated from my nursing course, my physical condition had not improved. I constantly coughed up blood, and even walking hurt. In 1978 at Moon Festival I received my nursing license. At that time the cancer had spread to my spine. I could only move my head and my arms. My lower body was helpless and at the same time very painful. It felt like needles constantly pricking me.

The doctor finally advised my parents to take me home. I had only two months to live. But my family wasn't willing to give up. They cared for me and were dedicated to seeing my recovery rather than just awaiting my death. I depended on them for everything, even for every sip of water.

But I despaired. What was the use of living like this? As time went on, suicide became an increasing temptation. I wanted to end my suffering and my hopeless life. And then the temptation passed, in a manner of speaking—I became physically incapable of carrying it out. I was in the depths of despair.

At that time there was a devout Christian intern who noticed my pitiful condition. He felt sorry for one so young having to face death, and he shared the gospel with me. But I wasn't interested. I didn't know there was a God or that he could help me. I certainly wasn't aware that I was a sinner.

No matter how busy this intern was, he came at least once a day to see me. This continued for some time. He'd often pray for me at my bedside. Gradually I became aware that the gospel he shared was full of peace, kindness, and comfort.

I remember two Bible verses he quoted. Psalm 46:1 was one: "God is our refuge and strength, a very present help in trouble" (KJV).

1 Corinthians 10:13 was the other: "No temptation has seized you except what is common to man. And God is faithful; he will not let you be tempted beyond what you can bear. But when you are tempted, he will also provide a way out so that you can stand up under it" (NIV).

As I was receiving chemotherapy, these verses were a great help to me. As soon as the anticancer drug entered my veins, I became terribly nauseated and vomited. My whole body rebelled. I often thought I couldn't stand it.

But I still remembered I wasn't alone. Somehow, God's word had entered my heart. I really knew that Jesus was bearing all of that pain with me. He was walking that long road with me.

You might say that I had no other choice, but I did learn the lesson of casting my burdens on Jesus. Also, during that time I learned to know myself. I realized I was a sinner. I learned humility and obedience. I found that the end of our human strength can be the beginning of God's strength and salvation.

On January 14, 1979, I was baptized in my bed in the hospital. The same year, in early February, a miracle happened. I began to move my toes. For half a year I constantly received physical therapy until finally I demonstrated my walking ability to my doctor.

At that time, 2 Corinthians 5:17 became significant to me. "If anyone is in Christ, he is a new creation; the old has gone, the new has come!"

My healing continued over the months. Eventually I returned to work. I am now the head nurse of the Ob-Gyn unit of the Mennonite Christian Hospital, and I have no evidence of my former illness.

The Lord also blessed me with a husband seven years ago. We have two young children—one age seven and one three years old.

Why did I experience so much suffering? I don't know, but in addition to restoring me, the Lord gave me an experience of suffering that makes me more able to empathize with others who suffer. Now as I take care of patients, I feel with them in their suffering.

Especially as patients face death or the possibility of being permanently handicapped, I know what it's like. I remember trying to deny my condition and its seriousness. The worry and fear are gone but not forgotten. I recall the depression and the anger and finally the acceptance. I can understand. For all this, I can really thank God. It is a gift.

The Night Birth

by Cora Lehman

Cora Lehman lives in Chambersburg, Pennsylvania. She served in Tanzania, Ethiopia, Somalia, and Kenya for twenty years with Eastern Mennonite Board of Missions. She has worked with maternal-child clinics, pediatrics, nursing education, and community health.

Jumping awake at the shrill ring of the phone in the early morning darkness, I groped for my flashlight.

The nights are cold at 8,000 feet in the mountains of Ethiopia. I shivered as I left behind my cozy bed with its layers of blankets. I went to the old-fashioned crank phone on the wall connecting me to the twenty-bed hospital and four main houses of what had been for twenty-six years the Deder Mennonite Mission Compound. This simple phone system had saved me many trips to the hospital—but not at 2:30 a.m. on this July 24, 1975.

When a voice from the hospital said, "An OB . . ." I seldom waited for more details about the woman in labor. The note of urgency in Solomon's voice spurred me to dress quickly. I put on my heavy sweater and wrapped myself—neck to knees—in my *gabi*, that snug blanket-sized wrap composed of multiple layers of soft, thin, gauzelike cotton worn by Ethiopians.

In the moonlight the peacefulness of the compound and the

valley below belied the turmoil of the nation. Ethiopia in 1975 was in ferment. The revolution was in full swing. And although it was just beginning to touch Deder community, change had already come to Deder Hospital.

In May 1975, the Mennonite Mission had turned the hospital over to the government. I had agreed to continue my services. But when the other nurse left on July 1, I was the only trained professional on the compound until the end of the month when Dr. Meldrum finally arrived.

Clutching my *gabi* about me on that cool July night, I glanced wistfully up the hill at the empty doctor's house. When would the promised doctor come? I wondered to myself. As usual, I prayed while hurrying along the hillside to the single story hospital and clinic building sprawled before me.

By the double-door entrance stood a lorry. It always gave me a sense of security to see that old truck there, available if transport to a larger hospital was needed. In remote areas, finding a vehicle was often difficult, but so was rounding up enough strong men to carry a patient on a makeshift stretcher many hours over mountainous paths. The more readily available transport of mules was not a suitable option for a woman in labor. Knowing these difficulties helped me to be less harsh on families who delayed too long in bringing their ailing ones for medical attention.

Entering the hospital, I exchanged the customary greetings briefly with the waiting *gabi*-clad family. Even by the pale light of their flickering kerosene lantern, their faces showed a mixture of anxiety and hope.

To the left of the short entrance corridor lay the small nurses' station, the treatment room, patient rooms, and two wards. I went beyond these rooms to the operating room which doubled as a delivery room. There on the simple operating table lay the patient. Even as I greeted her, I noted her small frame, so typically Ethiopian.

She politely returned the same Amharic greeting, meaning, "May he give you health."

"She's been in labor a long time," explained Solomon, the dresser (doctor's assistant) on duty.

"Her village is far from here," added Addiswerk, the aide, as he gently touched the young woman's hand.

I was continually impressed with the concern and compassion shown by these two young men. Our commitment to help this woman was first-class, but our combined expertise was less impressive. Solomon, no more than twenty years old, had one year of studying at the Dresser Bible School at Nazareth and some two years of hospital experience. Addiswerk, a few years younger, was an eager and dependable aide.

Although my nursing experience in Africa went back fourteen years, my experience delivering babies began only two years earlier with about fifty deliveries in nine months at Nazareth, Ethiopia. It continued at Deder. I was comfortable doing normal deliveries, even with episiotomies. But I lacked confidence with breech deliveries, and this petite little brown-skinned woman, I soon discovered, had a breech presentation.

On examination, I found my patient about ready to deliver! Likely that long ride over rough roads had worked in her favor, jostling the baby into position. She had labored long, but now, with our direction and encouragement, she pushed effectively and with good results.

I do believe that God inspired my memory as I vividly recalled the mechanics of breech deliveries illustrated in Margaret Myles' *Textbook for Midwives*. I also remembered other techniques explained to me, which I had used on several occasions.

Fortunately, the baby was small and the body easily delivered, including the arms and shoulders, in the prescribed manner. I allowed the weight of the body to bring the head into position. Then I was able to rotate the body upward, delivering the head and clearing the airway. A sense of God's presence helped me to work calmly.

As I held the baby up, I experienced a feeling of exhilaration, tempered, however, by concern for the infant's condition. Yes, there was *life*, and after some stimulation there was *breath*. The first feeble cry gradually strengthened, telling the tired mother that her labor was rewarded at last.

"Excuse me, Miss Cora. The lorry driver is asking permission to leave." Addiswerk rightly judged that this was an appropriate time to present this request.

"Well, okay," I conceded, thinking that with a living baby delivered the crisis was passed and what was to follow would be routine—simply delivering the placenta.

We had trained the staff to try to keep the vehicle which brought a patient until we could decide whether transport would be needed to a larger hospital. The nearest one was two hours away. Even when we decided that a case was beyond our abilities, families often hesitated to go elsewhere. The cost of transport was high and their financial resources meager. "Just do what you can," they would plead.

Their desperation often gave us courage to try (and there was no fear of a lawsuit). Sometimes doing what we could was not enough; the patient did not get well. Then the grieving family was almost apologetic that the patient had died in spite of our best efforts and the loving care they had witnessed.

The "just-do-what-you-can" dilemma was to become real to me that night. The minutes ticked by. I waited in vain for the lengthening of the cord and that little rush of blood which heralds the placenta's readiness to be delivered.

Give it time, I told myself, as I unsuccessfully tried the various techniques that on other occasions had seemed to help. I dared not tug too hard on the cord. The uterus might invert or the placenta would tear, leaving a large part of it inside with the danger of hemorrhage.

Finally, after nearly thirty minutes, I inserted my gloved hand all the way into the uterus. I found about one-fourth of the placenta firmly attached to the upper wall of the uterus.

"Placenta accreta, placenta accreta" began ringing in my ears. Try as I might, that placenta would not budge.

Praying fervently, I made a decision. I explained to my patient in Amharic that I would give her a rest. I added in English to my two supportive co-workers that I would leave the patient in their care while I went just down the hall to the doctor's office.

From the doctor's reference bookshelf, with the aid of my flashlight, I selected two obstetric texts. I searched for the section on *placenta accreta*. Alone in that cool quiet room, I kept praying for wisdom as I read. My sense of desperation was mixed with a little hope and a great faith that somehow God would see me through.

I noted the rarity of placenta accreta. Its treatment? "Hysterectomy!" Desperation increased. At 3:30 a.m., alone at Deder and with no transport, me do a hysterectomy?

I read on.

"Manual removal of the placenta." I knew it must be removed. The patient was slowly but surely losing blood. Because she had no prenatal care as we know it, I had no baseline by which to judge her initial physical condition. She seemed frail, but I had continually been amazed by the stamina of these mountain women.

Back in the operating room, seeing the trust in the eyes of my patient, I got to work with renewed hope and determination. No question about it, the placenta was still adhered. This time, following the textbook, I inserted my *left* hand into the uterus. I edged my fingers toward the part of the placenta adhering like velcro to the lining of the uterus.

The lone kerosene pressure light shown brightly near me as I carefully inched loose the grip of the placenta from the uterus. I was so intent on this tedious process that I was startled by the sound of Solomon's voice.

In a soft but intense voice he was asking, "Who sinned that we four have to suffer like this?" meaning himself, the aide, the patient, and me.

In some strange way, Solomon's declaration that he was also suffering made me feel somewhat less alone. As to this situation being a result of sin, I only briefly refuted the inferred premise. The topic would be seed for yet another of the many discussions between Solomon and me. I still treasure my memory of those talks, especially because within two years, this sensitive, talented youth became one of thousands senselessly mowed down as an "enemy of the revolution."

The agonizing process of loosening the placenta continued. "Finally," I wrote later in my diary, "with great difficulty, I got it out—one and a half hours after the baby was born."

The diary entry went on to tell of my getting a little sleep between 5:30 and 6:30 a.m. Then a busy day with another difficult delivery at noon: a first-time mother with hypertension and a huge hematoma of the labia caused by unskilled attempts at a home delivery.

That evening this second woman hemorrhaged, keeping me at the hospital until 10:00 p.m., when the bleeding was finally controlled. My concluding statement for July 24 was, "What a day! I survived with God's help."

And what of our brave little patient? She looked pale indeed, but I was still amazed to find that her hemoglobin was only 4.4 gm! (Mine was 15 gm!)

At Deder, blood transfusions were seldom done. While living elsewhere in malaria areas, I had drawn and transfused many units of blood (including my own). On this occasion we simply followed Deder's usual practice of giving several daily doses of intravenous iron followed by an oral iron preparation. Fortunately, the local grain was high in iron and an excellent blood builder.

Although I never had another contact with that special woman, she will always hold a place in my heart. So will the infant, whom the mother declared was not just her baby, but also belonged to me and God. This was her way of expressing extreme gratitude to both God and me.

AIDS Means Caring

by Lisa Busenitz

Lisa Busenitz is from Roanoke, Illinois. She has worked in intensive care units in several states as a traveling nurse.

In our rural setting we didn't see many cases of AIDS. I was aware that a lot of nurses I worked with were prejudiced about AIDS and didn't want to care for an AIDS patient. But within a year after I finished school, we had a patient come in who had AIDS, although he did not know when admitted that he had the disease. His family—a warm family, caring and close—had no idea he was homosexual.

The young man was admitted with respiratory problems. I think he had a premonition what was wrong with him, but it took a long time before he knew he had AIDS. Eventually he explained the situation to his parents, knowing that sooner or later they would find out anyway.

Several times I heard Larry say, "If there were anything I could do to take back that one moment, I would for anything."

Definitely not a promiscuous person, he alone did more for me in my attitude toward AIDS than anyone could have. He was kind and polite. I got to know his parents and his sister fairly well while taking care of him. I was able to build a rapport with them. They felt comfortable coming to me and asking questions about his condition. They could sense who cared.

I was with Larry and his mom when his pulmonologist told him that he was going to have to be intubated—a tube inserted for breathing—because he was having respiratory problems. The pulmonologist was caring and said, "We'll wait. What do you want to eat?" Larry's mom and sister went out and got him a sundae before the intubation, since it wasn't an emergency situation.

Larry was on the medical floor three months or more, and both his parents worked at the hospital. When I ran into them, I would ask how he was doing. Thus I was able to keep in contact even when I was working elsewhere. In the meantime, I had taken my ACLS (Advanced Cardiac Life Support) class. Then I heard that Larry had gone home, but had just been there for a day or so when he was readmitted, not doing well.

One night I was working on the medical floor when a "code" (emergency!) was called. "Running a code" meant quickly deciding what medication should be given, and when, and how; determining whether the patient should be defibrillated (shocked) to restore normal heart patterns; understanding and following certain protocols; coordinating the team efforts of several nurses and respiratory therapists, and the person watching the heart monitor.

This was my first code to run by myself. The adrenalin started pumping, I went running into the room—and it was Larry. I had never felt such a sinking feeling, realizing it was someone I knew and cared for. I couldn't just walk in and be detached, only doing my job.

Larry soon died, but caring didn't end there. I was able to be supportive to his parents after that too, when I would encounter them around the hospital. I think it made them feel good to know that someone remembered Larry even after he was gone, and that he had made an impact on my life, too.

Hug in a K-Mart

by Linda Kandel

Linda Kandel lives in Eureka, Illinois. She has worked in office nursing, operating room nursing, and day surgery/outpatient clinic (including some oncology). She volunteered as the school nurse for Hesston College for one year.

If someone asks me, "When did you practice nursing the way you wanted to?" I remember a patient I cared for a few years ago. I was working part time for two family practitioners and part time as a surgical nurse.

A patient came in to see the doctor, complaining of some rectal bleeding. The doctor examined him, did some blood work, and found that he was indeed anemic. The doctor decided he should see the gastroenterologist after having a colon X-ray.

I was the person who instructed the patient in the procedure and in the preparation. He had a barium enema, then later came back to the doctor and heard that there was a large tumor in the colon. I was with that patient when the doctor told him that it was probably malignant and he would need a colostomy.

I told the patient what this procedure would involve and was his nurse when he had the colonoscopy done at the hospital. A biopsy was done that same day. Back in the doctor's office the patient learned that, yes, the tumor was malignant. He needed surgery.

Because of my two jobs, I was the surgeon's nurse when this patient saw the surgeon in the clinic and we scheduled him for surgery. On the day of surgery I was the scrub nurse for his surgery. Because I work in a small hospital, I was also the recovery room nurse. I took care of him postoperatively each week as he came back to have the surgeon remove the staples from his incision.

During this ordeal, I felt able to give the family much support. I cried many times with his wife before and after the surgery. I was able to be the man's nurse when he came back six months later and had another colonoscopy, and this has gone on every six months since his initial surgery.

We see each other now in the grocery store and stop and talk. The last time we were at K-Mart, we embraced. Later my teenage daughter said, "What were you doing hugging that man in the store?"

I explained that this is what nursing is all about. This man is not just a patient, but a special person to me. And I like to think that I'm a special person to him and his family.

Walking Away with a Broken Back

by Katherine E. Yutzy

Katherine E. Yutzy lives in Goshen, Indiana. She spent seven and a half years in India with the Mennonite Board of Missions. She has worked with migratory families and in community health, nursing administration, and nursing education.

Close to the Mennonite hospital in India, a lot of new construction was being done. On each of these building sites many day laborers were employed—both men and women. In the middle of the afternoon on one particularly warm day, a nearly finished brick wall collapsed. Many injured workers were rushed to our hospital for emergency care.

It was well into the night before we finished the last cast on those with broken bones.

I had senior students working on the night shift, so I arrived early the next morning for the usual morning rounds with them. But when I entered the general ward for women, my students rushed up to me to say that one of the patients from the construction accident had left in the middle of the night.

"She was the last one to receive a cast last night. Remember?" they said. "She had fractured vertebrae and was told to stay flat on her bed. We were supposed to change her position every hour to help the plaster cast dry. But now she's gone!"

The students took me to her bed. Just as they said, the woman and all her possessions were gone—along with the family which had been there to support her. When I pulled back the top sheet, there was the woman's plaster cast, neatly unwrapped.

"We left everything just the way we found it," my students insisted. So I turned to some of the other patients in the vicinity and asked if they knew what had happened.

Several confirmed the story. Between the nurses' rounds, the woman's family had helped her unwrap the cast. She had walked out of the hospital on her own, bent over at the waist at a ninety-degree angle.

There was nothing to be done. The family came from a distant village and we never heard from them again. Every time I saw a lady walking in such a position I wondered if she was the one!

I later discovered that my Indian co-workers were sympathetic with this patient, for how could she live with a body cast? She could not sit. She could not even squat for elimination! For months she was destined to lie down or—when she became able—stand or walk if someone helped her up and down.

Was there something we should have done differently to fit into her culture? It had been Indian doctors who had applied the cast, but I hadn't thought of all the complications it would bring until we discussed it later. I came to realize that to really help people, one must consider much more than medical procedure.

The Keeping Room

by Jolene Hunsberger Schlosser

Jolene Hunsberger Schlosser lives in Quinton, Virginia. She worked as a charge nurse in Calico Rock, Arkansas, where she was in charge of all patients, including obstetrics, pediatrics, and medical-surgical. She has also worked in an extended care facility and home health.

Cool October breezes swept several unruly strands of hair around my face as I headed toward the Calico Rock Medical Center for another day shift. The short walk was always an invigorating way to start the day, especially since the colors of autumn were lingering around me as I made the last turn up Grasse Street. It was over a year now since I had moved to beautiful, rural Calico Rock, Arkansas, to begin my nursing career.

After initial greetings and some small talk, duty began in earnest. A young, single woman in early labor had arrived in the clinic at 6:30 a.m. As I prioritized my day, I knew it would be busy. Our thirty-bed hospital was small but certainly not without excitement.

As I navigated the hall between breakfast carts, housekeepers, and other hospital staff, I pondered the plight of this young, single woman facing labor and delivery. Our ages were similar.

And I too was single, though not pregnant. I wondered how she was coping. My own values and a desire to live a life "hidden with Christ" rose to awareness as I reminded myself that what she probably needed was care and compassion.

Upon entering the clinic area, I was greeted by Beverly, coach and widowed mother of my labor and delivery patient. She was petite and dignified. Later her endless energy proved a real asset during the birthing process.

Being a great conversationalist, Beverly immediately introduced herself to me. Her daughter Valerie, less verbal but just as vibrant, answered the routine admission questions. I wheeled Valerie to the labor room to finish taking vital signs and checking fetal heart tones.

As charge nurse, I had many other responsibilities but periodically checked in on Valerie. During these checks, we continued to chat, and Valerie's story began to unfold.

This attractive black-haired, brown-eyed woman had met a young college peer with whom she had gotten pregnant. She did not want to marry him. She had received routine college counseling regarding getting an abortion. But after thinking it over, Valerie decided an abortion was not a viable option for her. "I just couldn't do that. It's murder."

During her pregnancy, she tried to take good care of herself, and Beverly helped by cooking nutritious meals. Valerie then made the decision to give her baby up for adoption.

She commented, "The baby will have a better life with someone else since I'm not married and don't know how to take care of a baby."

Her mother and married sisters supported her decision. Between contractions and breathing, I listened, asked questions at times, trying to be a supportive professional. At the same time a friendship was budding.

As my shift progressed, labor slowly increased. But at 3:30 p.m. it was time for me to bid Valerie good-bye and hope all would go well.

The following day, when I reported back for a 3:00-11:00 p.m. shift, I was astonished to learn that Valerie's labor had slowed the previous day. Now it was active again due to medication given to start her labor.

When I went to join Valerie, her family exclaimed, "That baby just waited for you to come back to the hospital!"

And so she had, because on October 21, 1979, after 8:00 p.m., the little seven-pound, three-ounce baby was delivered.

Valerie asked about her child, and I softly said, "You had a beautiful baby girl."

However, as instructed by Dr. Milam, I was not to show this dark-haired wonder to her mother. The theory at that time was that bonding time between mother and child would only make it harder to follow through with the adoption. But curious grandma stole a peek. My tears blurred the way to the nursery. I could only wonder if this innocent bundle of sweetness would ever realize how much her birth mother cared about her.

After the stitching and other postpartum care was finished, Valerie was taken to the medical-surgical area of our hospital out of respect for her desire not to keep the baby. At 11:30 p.m. I bid good-bye once more.

Valerie is a brave young woman, I thought as I started home. Her long, difficult labor and delivery had been exhausting both to the new mother and her family. I was glad that Baby Shortt had finally arrived.

However, a new surprise awaited me when I returned to work the next day. During the twenty-four-hour waiting period required by law before a birth mother signs the documents to give up her baby, Valerie had changed her mind. She decided that she was capable of loving and caring for her precious new daughter. And her mother and extended family promised to help her with this new responsibility, which seemed overwhelming to Valerie.

Valerie notified the social worker of her decision. Then the new mother was moved back to her old room, since in our small hospital the same room is used for the entire labor and postpartum stay.

Valerie now needed a name for her baby. She chose Miranda, a character from the primitive art painting hung in her labor room, for the first name. Dr. Meryl and Gladys Grasse always displayed interesting local art throughout the hospital, including this painting by the late Essie Ward.

The middle name came as a special treat to me—Jolene. I couldn't have been more pleased. Rocking my little namesake in the nursery became extra special, and my prayer was that she would one day experience the love of Jesus in her heart.

Soon it was time to prepare them for homegoing. One last sweep around the room for stray articles gave me a chance to catch another glimpse of Miranda, the spicy Ozark Mountain character frozen in time in that painting. The rhythm of her name linked with mine sounded just right for this new little life leaving this special room, which I thought of as the Keeping Room.

The road over which Valerie had traveled hadn't been easy. We all knew her new responsibility would make it even more. But Miranda Jolene, affectionately known as Randy Jo, did go home with her mom after all!

I Can't Do It for Her

by Lois Lehman

Lois Lehman lives in Kirkwood, Pennsylvania. She served four years with Indian Health Service in Alaska doing community health nursing. She is a nurse midwife and has worked on the Rosebud Indian Reservation in South Dakota and at home births and birthing centers in Pennsylvania.

My two children and I stepped from the jet. Wind swept across the Alaskan tundra, penetrating our summer jackets. We had arrived in Bethel to visit my friend Sandy and her son Robert.

We waited for our luggage. Ten-year-old Christopher and fourteen-year-old Angela huddled close to me. No one came forward to meet us, but I had Sandy's house number written on one of her recent letters.

Finally, a man with a pickup asked if we needed a lift to town. He kindly loaded our stuff in the back, and we crowded into the cab. I told him the address, and soon we pulled up to a house that looked like each of the other seventy-five or so houses nearby. Picking up sleeping bags and suitcases we climbed the sand-strewn steps and knocked. All three of us were trembling on the verge of a new experience.

After communicating only by letter for ten years, Sandy and I were meeting again. The door opened slowly. Sandy, an Alas-

103

kan native, overweight, in her early thirties, stood there. We said, "Hi," and went in.

"I'm nervous!" Sandy said.

"Me too!"

We laughed, relieved.

Slowly we began visiting. The kids and I planned to stay with her three weeks before going up river. We'd sleep in Robert's room on the floor (no bed), and we'd do the cooking and laundry (wringer washer).

Sandy, after being on the waiting list for ever so long, had finally been able to rent this house. It was a victory for her to move from the house of her brother and father. We talked of her new commitment to sobriety—soon to be a one-year celebration.

I had first met Sandy in 1973 when I worked for the U.S. Public Health Service Hospital in Alaska. Sandy had been a "patient with a human bite," but she was also in need of simple friendship. Our conversation had often been one-sided—my side—but that was okay.

When I transferred to State of Alaska Public Health Nursing, I visited Sandy in her home by the Kuskokwim River on official home visits. Baby Robert (Goony he was called) was a chubby Eskimo baby. I offered suggestions on child care, nutrition, and encouraged immunizations.

One lesson I learned in those early days of friendship—never think people don't care about their houses even if things seem messy. Sandy's house shocked me. Surrounding it were piles of garbage and frozen soiled clothes. There was an open honey bucket in the shed. Things looked only slightly better within.

But then one day I overheard Sandy complaining that visitors had thrown candy wrappers on the floor. At first I thought, *What difference does it make in all this mess!* Then I realized all of us have our own standards, our own difficulties with housekeeping, and our own pride.

Sandy was serious about friendships with *gussick* (white) women. Other friends who had left Bethel had stopped writing to her. "They don't write even though I write to them," Sandy said.

This prompted me to make a silent commitment to write her when I left Alaska. I kept the commitment. Sandy's questions made writing letters to her easy. She wanted to know what my family ate, how the house was arranged, how many animals we had at our Pennsylvania place, and so forth.

I enjoyed her letters. She wrote more than she talked; on paper she freely shared her ups and downs and the happenings around Bethel. She also explained that her mother's drinking had finally caused her father to move out of the house into a cabin he had built for himself directly behind the family house. There he lived alone and kept it locked whenever he was away. Finally her mother died, and she mentioned that her brother and father were also alcoholic.

For years Sandy didn't admit her own drinking problem. It was there in her letters—"I broke my glasses and had to go hospital for another pair"—but she never admitted what caused such mishaps. Then one day she wrote that she was entering alcohol rehabilitation. Later came a letter telling that she was getting into her own housing, and finally the time seemed ripe for a visit: 1986.

In Sandy's "new" house, we visited until midnight and it was still daylight. I had to hang rags over the bedroom windows so Angela and Christopher could get to sleep even though there were dogs barking and children crying outside.

Sandy and I sat at the table sharing in low voices. She told of the circumstances surrounding Robert's conception and birth. She admitted her fears of the future when he became sixteen and she would no longer receive aid for dependent children.

I encouraged her to get her GED (high school equivalent degree). "It could really lead to a lasting job," I said.

She said that she had mostly gussick friends. Her native friends drank, and she needed to maintain a distance to keep her sobriety. Inwardly I cried for her.

After I returned to the "lower forty-eight," we continued to write regularly for a while, but by the fall of 1988 several months has passed with no letter from Sandy. I was uneasy.

Finally one came: *How can it be, dear God? She's drinking again, and pregnant! Have I failed in praying and support across the thousands of miles?*

Sandy was afraid. She drank through the pregnancy. She was drunk at the delivery of her premature baby girl. Social Services took the child away but allowed visiting privileges as long as Sandy was sober.

In the winter of 1990, Sandy wrote to say that she no longer had visiting privileges. She was angry.

What can I say? To myself I repeat, "Let us not become weary in doing good, for at the proper time we will reap a harvest if we do not give up" (Gal. 6:9) and "Pray continually" (1 Thess. 5:17). I realize Sandy's responsibility in getting her life together. It's something I cannot do for her.

A Lesson About Stereotyping

by Carolyn Peachey Rudy

Carolyn Peachey Rudy lives in La Junta, Colorado. She has worked in labor/birth, and office nursing. She served three years in Somalia with Mennonite Central Committee working with refugees.

It was one of those nights! The evening shift's report in this Colorado hospital compelled me to get myself organized quickly or I would never catch up with all I had to do. My plan was to count the narcotics, set out the paperwork and review medications to be given. *Then* I would do a quick check on my patients—with an emphasis on *quick*.

I headed toward the birthing room, remembering the shift report. "A forty-five-year-old pregnant mother of three with two living; last pregnancy was twelve years ago; single mother; short and stocky build; admitted this morning due to decreased fetal movement."

The obstetrician tried, without much success, to induce labor with medication later in the day. Now the Pitocin drip was turned off for the night in hopes that the patient would get some sleep. The evening nurses had given her a sleeping pill and reported that she was resting.

The fact that this patient, though older, was a single parent must have triggered my thoughts about all the single, teenage moms I had worked with. I felt discouraged as I slipped into the darkened room. Would this be yet another case of an unplanned pregnancy where the father is not involved?

I could hear the steady "thump, thump, thump" of the baby's heart beat on the monitor. Eventually I could see the woman's shape on the bed. Her eyes were wide open, so I asked how it was going.

"I'm too hot," she complained. "The bed is too hard. And I want something to drink."

After a quick check of the monitor tracing, I opened a few doors for circulation and told the woman I would bring her some hot tea.

Just go to sleep, lady, I thought as I rushed out of the room toward the kitchenette. The last thing I needed right now was a demanding patient. At least the birthing room was away from the noises of the nurses' station. That should aid her sleeping. Even though the tracing had showed a few contractions, the patient hadn't seemed to notice them.

One hour later as I was making rounds again, a sobbing noise came from the birthing room. *Perhaps the contractions are getting harder*, I thought as I pushed open the door. I laid my hand on her arm and asked if she was having some pain.

She denied any labor pains but said her back was so sore from lying in bed. The sleeping pill had not even touched this person. She quickly accepted my offer of a back rub, and this was when her whole story came out.

She began by saying she was lonely and missed her family. She had a sixteen-year-old son and twelve-year-old daughter living with her parents in another state. The father of these two children had been her husband at one time, but he had died young, leaving her to raise the children on her own. The loss was deep, so deep that for years she hadn't permitted herself to even think of remarriage.

But in the midst of her pain, her extended family had been

supportive and close. Actually, she was now pregnant because their love had finally softened her defenses and she had allowed herself to believe in a man again. Her boyfriend had wanted her to move to his hometown, and she had done so four months earlier. She found his parents mean and hard to live with. She had planned to return home to have the baby, but then, due to complications, she had stayed in town.

She basically had no support group except for one prodigal sister of her boyfriend. She had purposely kept the news regarding her pregnancy complications from her own family so they wouldn't worry. Now here she was with nonprogressive labor and the possibility of a cesarean section the next day.

My heart went out to this lonely woman. Suddenly my prejudices were dashed to the ground. My mind groped for solutions. Would it help for her to call her family long distance? But that was not much of an option in the early morning hours. Could she ask her boyfriend's sister to come to the hospital tomorrow? That might work. She agreed and said she would call the sister in the morning.

As I finished the back rub, she was no longer crying. I humbly realized that this person simply needed someone to do more than just check the monitor tracings and IV solution every half hour. She needed someone to listen to her and to give her some physical contact as well. I thought of how easy it is to put our own needs for organization and efficiency ahead of our patients' needs for a little undivided attention.

A few nights and a c-section later, I found this mother walking around the halls with her little baby in her arms. She was beaming into the face of the child she had named to mean "a gift from God."

I was truly touched as I watched this woman who had had so many hard knocks in life. She reminded me of an angel of peace as she quietly slipped into other patients' rooms to chat a bit when she noticed they could not sleep. She also encouraged the first-time mothers as she recounted tips learned from raising her first two children.

She is gone from the unit now, but her lesson to me has remained behind. Although stereotyping is still easy to do, now I think twice about it.

A Grain of Wheat

by Gertrude Friesen

Gertrude Friesen lives in Swan River, Manitoba. She has worked as a staff nurse in obstetrics. She has served at several small hospitals in Manitoba on all units and all shifts.

"Help! She's stopped breathing." The cry escaped my lips just as we were approaching the town of Dauphin. I screamed, "Oh no, Murray, she's not breathing!"

Less than two hours before, the ambulance had left Swan River Hospital speeding toward Winnipeg with four-year-old Tammie, who was critically ill.

Earlier that morning I had begun the day shift on the pediatric ward. Tammie had been admitted during the night with severe diarrhea and had slipped into unconsciousness. Her young native parents anxiously hovered over her.

After the spinal tap revealed no abnormalities, plans were made to send Tammie to Winnipeg by ambulance. It was the weekend and difficult to find a registered nurse to accompany the child. I offered to go with the ambulance even though two hours of my regular shift remained.

Tammie's mother, Wilma, a quiet, soft-spoken mother of four, sat next to her unconscious daughter for the five-hour ride to Winnipeg.

"Don't spare the Valium," said the concerned doctor as we

prepared to depart. "We don't want her to convulse."

Murray, the ambulance driver, shut the back door and got behind the steering wheel. "Everything okay?" he asked, then flicked on the flashing amber-and-red lights and sped away.

The first hour and a half were uneventful. Then Tammie began to stir. She hadn't had any medication for several hours, so I carefully injected a small amount of Valium into the IV tubing.

Several minutes passed. An icy fear gripped my heart. "Is she breathing?" I whispered to myself, hoping Wilma hadn't noticed. I couldn't find a pulse. Tammie's face became deathly pale. I began CPR immediately.

Lorne, the assistant driver, asked Wilma to trade places with him. The mother kept her eyes on the child as Lorne and I worked. Murray radioed the Dauphin Hospital that we were coming and gave an estimated time of arrival of three minutes. When we arrived at the hospital, the resuscitation team was waiting for us. The stretcher was quickly unloaded and disappeared down the hall to one of the emergency rooms.

Forty minutes later, despite the heroic efforts of the staff, Tammie's little heart refused to beat.

While all this activity was going on, Wilma and I waited quietly in a small room nearby. I quoted Bible verses and prayed fervently for Tammie's life. The doctor came to our room. I saw tears in his eyes.

He walked over to Wilma and me and said, "I'm sorry, but we could not bring her back." He took Wilma's hand in his and said, "We did everything we could!"

Then he turned to me, "Nurse, will you be okay?" I assured him I would be and watched him slowly walk away.

I hugged Wilma and kissed her. Our tears mingled as we wept over the little life that was no more. A priest was called. When he came, he spoke words of comfort to the grieving mother.

Papers were signed releasing Tammie's body for an autopsy.

Then we were on our way back to Swan River, carrying an empty stretcher with a crumpled blanket.

As we approached Swan River a severe thunderstorm raged, with torrents of rain and jagged flashes of lightning adding to the horror of the last few hours. I got drenched dashing from the ambulance to my car.

I turned on the ignition and immediately the tape in the cassette player filled the car with music and the beautiful words from 1 Chronicles 29:11, "Yours, O Lord, is the greatness and the power and the glory . . . ." Tears coursed down my cheeks as the windshield wipers groaned while trying to clear the heavy rain from the window. I could hardly see to drive.

Later that year an elderly native woman and I drove to the Pelican Rapids Reserve to see Wilma. I took some books for Wilma and her children. She was so glad to see me. It was good to see her husband again, too, and she eagerly introduced me to her other children.

A year later I met Wilma on the maternity ward. She had given birth to twins, a boy and a girl.

I have corresponded with Wilma from time to time. A few years ago I heard from a friend that she and her husband had become Christians and were planning to come to Swan River gospel meetings. I was excited to hear this and looked forward to meeting them after not seeing them for several years.

A smiling bespectacled lady in a lovely white suit stood at the open door. Her radiant face spoke of the peace within. She recognized me first, and we flew into each other's arms!

Later, when I asked her what made her first consider the Lord Jesus, she replied, "I kept thinking of Tammie and where she was. When she died you said she was in heaven with Jesus. I wanted to see her again, so I had to find the way."

I remembered the words of Jesus. "I tell you the truth, unless a kernel of wheat falls to the ground and dies, it remains only a single seed. But if it dies, it produces many seeds."

Pastoring Body and Soul

by Linda Witmer

Linda Witmer lives in Goshen, Indiana. She served with Mennonite Central Committee in Guatemala for nine years with the Health Promoter Program. She has done community health and nursing education.

While Debbie Yoder and I were in Guatemala working with the Kekchi Indians, we developed a curriculum for educating village health workers. We taught health workers who were chosen by their communities to provide basic preventative and curative health care in their own village. The promoters were licensed by the government and their work was seen as an extension of the church.

Pedro was one of these village health workers.

Within the small village of Santa Cecilia is a Mennonite church, with an attendance of about fifty people, mostly Kekchi Indians. This church chose Pedro to be their pastor and health promoter. At nineteen years of age, Pedro accepted those responsibilities with enthusiasm.

When we first met Pedro, he had the low self-esteem typical of most Kekchi people who have not had formal education. He felt powerless, inferior, unable to learn. He saw his life stretch out before him, saw himself doomed to the same meager existence as generations before him.

Most of the Kekchi Indians in the health promoters class had taught themselves to read. When Pedro finished the class he told us, "I never knew a Kekchi person could be a health worker."

I told him, "It's not that you are dumb, just that now you have had the opportunity."

On Thursdays it was possible to see Pedro in action in his small clinic. He spent time with his patients and explained to them not only their sicknesses, but how they had contracted them and how to prevent them. Once a month he weighed the babies in his village and taught the mothers when to introduce new foods to their children.

On Sundays he preached to his small congregation. About once a month he included a health lesson in his church service. The subject could have been nutrition, sanitation, or child care. As he taught, the whole congregation was involved in discussing illnesses and their prevention.

In his own home, Pedro spent many hours teaching his own parents about health. He helped them understand that some of their traditional ways of doing things weren't wise. Pedro's mother had ten children, only four of whom lived.

When his mother gave birth to a baby girl, the only female who lived, she became a dearly loved child. When the baby was six months old, Pedro explained to his mother the importance of introducing new foods carefully and what kinds of food his little sister needed to prevent malnutrition.

Pedro explained the importance of having the baby vaccinated to prevent childhood diseases. Some of the other children in the family had died from measles and whooping cough. Although Pedro's parents did not understand all the new ideas Pedro introduced, they trusted him and tried to make changes in their home.

Once Pedro's six-year-old brother contracted measles and pneumonia. His mother gave Pedro full responsibility for taking care of his sick brother. Pedro stayed up all night administering medicine and praying for his little brother until the fever broke. By God's grace, his brother lived.

Over lunch break or after supper, Pedro had the habit of teaching reading to church members as well as other people in the community. One week every two months for three years he went to Carcha to study at the Bible institute.

Pedro's work as pastor and health promoter helped him change his attitude about life for himself and his people. He learned that he had choices and could help others make choices. Education about health was power for change.

Why was Pedro so dedicated to his people? Christ made the difference in his life. Through studying, Pedro gained a new understanding of who he was and the potential the Kekchi people have. He no longer had a fatalistic attitude toward life as did so many of his people.

Pedro received new life and freedom in Christ. Even though he experienced much injustice and oppression from the government, he was not in bondage. He had hope not only for himself but also for his people.

Crossing Over

by Mary L. Weaver

Mary L. Weaver lives in Bluffton, Ohio. She has done staff nursing and nursing administration in an extended care facility. She also served in Algeria and Germany.

Hannah was in her nineties, a slender, wiry, white-haired woman living on the nursing unit of our retirement home. She did not *seem* old. She walked quickly, read a great deal, and expressed opinions on almost every topic. She was a retired missionary who had served many years in foreign countries, a situation that demanded resourcefulness.

When Hannah was asked to give the noon prayer in our dining room at the home, she rarely simply prayed. She usually stood by her chair and addressed the others, challenging them to think about some current issue. Then she prayed, intensely.

Hannah was not afraid of death and spoke of it often to me and the other nurses. She anticipated heaven, seeing the Lord face to face, and rejoining others who died before her, especially her husband.

Hannah passionately wanted to die in her room, with the caring staff she knew, with her family by her side if possible. She hoped her death would not be painful. But she requested not to be hospitalized at the end of life. She did not want her life prolonged with invasive measures. She was dictating her own "Plan of Care."

As months went by, Hannah's body deteriorated. Her mind remained sharp, but her responses slowed as death approached. Our goal as a nursing staff was to carry out her wishes, to help Hannah have the "good death" she so clearly outlined for us.

In her final days, Hannah was cared for by staff who had grown to love her. The nursing assistants and nurses provided wonderful supportive care. They kept her body clean and lotioned, gave her sips of liquid by mouth, repositioned her every two hours or more frequently around the clock, provided good oral care, moistened her drying lips, relieved her pain, and spoke softly to her while caring for her.

Soft taped music played at the bedside at intervals, promoting a relaxed atmosphere. We knew Hannah's taste in music because we knew Hannah. In the last week of her life Hannah told me that her husband came in the room at night. "He tweaks my toes and makes me smile," she snickered.

She seemed at such peace with herself. Her ministers visited her and gave her spiritual support.

Hannah's family was supportive throughout her stay at the home and came to be with Hannah during her final hours. They sat by the bedside, holding her hand or touching her arm, speaking infrequently.

By then Hannah was no longer speaking. The nursing staff cared for her without requesting the family to leave the room. The family was comfortable with that arrangement. I checked in frequently, assessing Hannah for pain and the progression of her end-of-life process. I checked with the family to see if I could help them in any way, trying to be sensitive to their need for me to stay in the room or to be alone with their mother.

When the end came, Hannah's son and daughter-in-law were holding her right hand. I held the other one. They were crying softly as soft hymns of faith played in the background.

"Would you like a little time to be with her alone?" I asked.

They would. I pulled the curtain to give them privacy and assisted Hannah's roommate to another comfortable area in the home.

"Hannah's gone now," I told the roommate.

The family remained with the body as long as they wished. There was no reason to call the funeral home immediately. I continued with all my phone calls and necessary paperwork. As the family left, I joined them for a walk in the hall.

The nursing assistants lovingly washed Hannah's body one last time. They lay her flat on the bed, her head on a small pillow, and pulled the covers neatly to midchest. Her body was treated with great respect.

After the funeral director came and removed Hannah's body, I escorted Hannah's roommate back to her room arm-in-arm. We talked about Hannah, what a lively person she was, how she cared about the issues in the church, how much we would miss her. I settled Hannah's roommate in her easy chair and turned to leave.

"Wait," she said.

I turned to look directly into the woman's eyes.

"I hope you are here when I die."

An Easter Reflection from El Salvador

by Susan Classen

Susan Classen lives in San Salvador, El Salvador. She served three years in Bolivia and several years in El Salvador with Mennonite Central Committee.

Lies, deceit, and falsehood are in power in El Salvador while truth agonizes on the cross. When, in this war-torn country, will truth be resurrected in its liberating glory?

I identify with the prophet Isaiah's pronouncement: "Truth has stumbled in the streets, honesty cannot enter. Truth is nowhere to be found, and whoever shuns evil becomes a prey" (Isa. 59:14-15). A Chilean bishop summed it up well when he said, "Those who commit the crimes go free, while those who denounce them are persecuted."

It was 1:00 a.m. on Good Friday morning while these and many other thoughts whirled through my head. I was in the back of a pickup truck with Francisco, a seventeen-year-old villager who had been injured by a grenade. Fransisco's father was up front, driving.

One person had been killed and three others injured by a grenade left behind by government soldiers. Francisco's life had been saved by an emergency operation performed on the spot by a guerrilla doctor. We were on our way to the hospital.

My fears of the risk involved in helping him receive adequate medical care had already been confirmed. At 9:30 the night before, five hours into the agonizingly long trip over washed-out dirt roads, we had been stopped at an army checkpoint.

When the soldiers saw the hammock strung in the back of the truck, their first question was, "Is the patient a man or woman?"

Hearing that he was a man, they immediately sent us to their commanding officer, since young men are suspected of being guerrillas. We were detained for two hours as they debated what should be done. All the while the uneven rhythm of Francisco's labored breathing echoed in my ears. Finally the officer let us go, but by that time it was 11:45 p.m., and the road was abandoned. Salvadorans know better than to be out at night.

Soon after 1:00 a.m., when we finally arrived at the hospital, I understood why we had been permitted to continue. Soldiers accosted us the moment we pulled in. They had been radioed to expect us.

As soon as I jumped off the truck, I was pulled aside for questioning. "Who are you? Who do you work for? What happened to this man? Where is he from?" The questions went on and on.

The soldiers informed Francisco's father that his son was under custody. He would be watched while he was in the hospital, and then he would be taken for investigation.

The accusations, while unspoken, were clearly communicated. Francisco was thought to be a guerrilla because he was a young man injured by a grenade. I was a guerrilla sympathizer because I brought him in for medical care. The fact that Francisco had been operated on by a guerrilla doctor seemed to confirm these suspicions as far as the military was concerned.

For the next twenty-four hours, I reviewed over and over my decision to take Francisco to the public hospital. If we had gone to a private clinic, we probably could have avoided the confrontation with the soldiers in the hospital.

But part of me rebelled at the thought of hiding Francisco in a private hospital. After all, the truth was on our side. Francisco was a young peasant farmer injured in a tragic accident. I was a church worker doing my best to help those in need no matter what their political persuasion. And international law guarantees the right to medical treatment regardless of whether the doctor happens to be a guerrilla.

But it was still a grim Good Friday for the truth in El Salvador. Innocence is not presumed in the middle of any civil war. And those who proclaim the truth take a real risk. Meanwhile we live with the hope that truth will ultimately triumph as we faithfully proclaim it in whatever situations we encounter.

It Hurts—Fix It

by Beckie Rice Smucker

Beckie Rice Smucker lives in Phoenix, Arizona. She is a head nurse of an operating room. In West Sierra Leone she was a nurse for missionary children. She served in the Dominican Republic.

A patient came into the emergency room with a dissecting aortic aneurism. An aneurism is a blood vessel wall that separates and balloons. A dissecting aortic aneurism hemorrhages from a split in the vessel wall. Unable to breathe well, the patient was being ventilated while being prepared for the surgery without which he would die.

The family said, "He's depressed. He's tried suicide twice in the past year and always said, 'If anything happens, leave me.' "

I hurried upstairs to the heart room and found the nursing supervisor. "We should wait before opening everything up," I said. "If this is what they want, we shouldn't operate. He's still conscious, you know, and in pain."

I told the doctor what the family told me. He said he needed to pursue this. I went with the doctor to the patient's bedside.

The doctor explained, "You have a blowout in your blood vessel that we need to fix. There is a 20 percent chance that we can't fix the problem. Do you want us to go ahead?"

He wrote on a pad, "It hurts."

The doctor said, "I know it hurts. We can do something for the pain. But do you want us to go ahead with the surgery?"

The man wrote, "It hurts. Fix it!"

Despite all his troubles, when it got down to the bottom line, he didn't want to die. Surgery was successful.

We didn't do any kind of follow-up on this person. Sometimes I wonder if when he went home he tried suicide again. I don't know . . . but I doubt it.

Patient Advocate

by Lisa Busenitz

Lisa Busenitz is from Roanoke, Illinois. She has worked in intensive care units in several states as a traveling nurse.

I was working in Illinois with a patient who was obviously terminal, a young woman who only had one child. Her family was very supportive, but a lot of the nurses were intimidated by having a family in the intensive care unit. In the ICU a family was restricted to visiting for ten minutes every two hours. But since this patient was terminal, it had been decided that her family could stay longer.

The family was frustrated with these visiting policies. They felt like they couldn't visit freely in the room since other patients were there, too. Another patient's family wondered why they couldn't be in the room also.

The dying young woman was made a "no-code" (no resuscitation) but couldn't be moved to a regular unit because she was on intravenous medications. I found this frustrating because the IV didn't need special care. If her blood pressure would bottom out, we weren't going to increase the drugs. Still, the regular units didn't want the specialized medications.

I worked with the family, doctors, and house supervisors to get this patient transferred out to the unit and finally succeeded. I had not been such an assertive nurse before.

The family was appreciative. They were especially thankful because they then felt comfortable staying with the patient until she died several days later. It was better for them to have time with her without nurses constantly hovering around, as they tend to do in an ICU.

I found the role of patient advocate to be truly rewarding.

The Light in the Dark

by Evonne Lu and Dianna Eshleman

Evonne Lu lives in Hualien, Taiwan. She is the director of nursing for Mennonite Christian Hospital in Hualien.

Dianna Eshleman lives in Salem Oregon. She served two years with General Conference Mennonite Commission on Overseas Mission in Taiwan. She has worked mostly in obstetrics and intensive nursery and volunteered in a community prenatal clinic.

Wong, a sixty-seven-year-old man who had worked for forty years as a mechanical engineer in Taiwan, was admitted to the Mennonite Christian Hospital in Hualien, Taiwan, on February 5, 1990. He had generalized edema (swelling from excessive fluid retention) and pain in his right leg due to deep vein thrombosis (a blood clot). Despite therapy with a medication to prevent blood coagulation, amputation was necessary on February 10.

The surgeon followed Wong's request for a below-the-knee rather than midthigh amputation, despite a better prognosis for healing the stump. Wong appreciated the surgeon allowing him to take the risk.

Between the time when Wong was first admitted and when the decision was made regarding surgery, the nursing staff told him repeatedly that they were praying for him. "Even if you are not a Christian, we can still pray for you," said a young student nurse.

Wong, who had been raised in a traditional Buddhist family, equated worshiping God with worshiping his ancestors. He had resisted the efforts of his daughter to go to church since her conversion to Christianity while a student at Mennonite Christian Hospital's nursing school many years before. But he admits that his family's support and knowing people were praying helped him to accept the difficult ordeal of amputation.

The operation went well, but three days later Wong showed signs of shock. Upper GI bleeding due to the heparin therapy was suspected. The effects of shock caused Wong to become mentally disoriented. His daughter had to give permission for emergency surgery.

In the intensive care unit after surgery, he indicated to his daughter (by flexing his index finger—a Taiwanese gesture) that he felt he was dying. His daughter reassured him that he was *not*. She told her father that her church in Taipei as well as Christian friends in Hualien were praying earnestly for him.

And then, while he was on the critical list, he had an experience he is still trying to understand. Everything was dark for him except for a line of bright light going from his head. He felt very tired but couldn't sleep. The light weakened and almost went out. Then suddenly it became bright, and his mind felt peaceful.

He has struggled to understand this special experience as he has recovered. What was it? What did it mean? He doesn't know—but it has made him to want to understand who Jesus Christ is. He's not yet ready to be baptized, but reads the Bible and attends church.

He often tells people about his experience, emphasizing that it's hard at his age to make so big a change as becoming a Christian. With the exception of one daughter, his whole family has been traditionally Buddhist, practicing ancestor worship. For many years he had resisted the entreaties of his daughter and Christian friends. Christ was okay for them but not him. Now, however, he wants to learn more about Christ. His wife also wants to attend church.

"Why would so many people pray for me?" he wonders.

Long-Term Care

by Susan Kehler

*Susan Kehler lives in Sumas, Washington. She is the director of
nursing of a long-term care facility in Canada. She served
twenty-three years in Taiwan with General Conference Commission on Overseas Mission, where she started a school
of nursing.*

Long-term care facilities are often viewed as doing nursing
in the "slow lane." Yet it is not just speed that represents true
caring.

Sandy had a history of turmoil and trouble. She told me she
had been abused by her husband (who then divorced her).
Physicians diagnosed her as manic-depressive in a "controlled" state. The long-term care assessors said, "We doubt
that you'll have any behavioral-management problems with
her, but if you do, you can always readmit her to the psych unit
at the acute care hospital."

She'd spent a great deal of time there already. We did calcu-
lated planning and wrote a letter to her physician, solic-
iting—and receiving—his eager cooperation.

The day came. Sandy arrived, with her darting eyes, irritable
behavior, yelling at nurses in the middle of the night, demanding, and endless pacing. We talked. We made care plans. She
made promise after promise to improve. Her physician kept

helping by personal visits, pleading, threatening. The long-term care assessors kept phoning.

This all seemed like concerted cooperation. True—but there were also other nurses who privately threatened to resign unless we could get rid of her. "She doesn't belong here," they objected. I couldn't argue that, but where did she belong? She had no home. Was a psych hospital to be her permanent dumping place?

I bargained with the staff. Give her a few weeks. Maybe she'll blend into the depressive phase. Then came the deadline for deciding what should happen to her. Much prayer went up for wisdom. What would it be? I dared to share the Monday morning report with the long-term care staff. Sandy had been much more settled. The long-term care assessor responded, "You said you'd pray. Is this the answer, that you think we should keep her?"

Happily, the head nurse of the unit was understanding. Sandy stayed.

Soon thereafter Sandy informed us, "I want to stay here if you'll let me. I know you people love me."

She's still not always a model of good behavior, but she's "in." We love her and she loves us.

Learning to Love Doc

by Arleta M. Martin

Arleta M. Martin lives in Hagerstown, Maryland. She has worked as the head nurse of a pediatrics unit for more than twenty years.

It was the first day of anatomy class. The instructor marched into the classroom, stood at the head of the class, and observed us for awhile. Then she stated, "Half of you are too smart to be here. The other half will fail. You won't pass the first exam."

Well, I did fail that first exam, as did the majority of the class. Discouraged, we called home to tell our families the sad news. Despite our difficulties, however, at least three-quarters of the class ultimately succeeded (although anatomy and physiology was never a favorite subject).

That classroom experience was my first encounter with Doc, as our instructor, not too affectionately, was known. I learned to fear and respect her. Over the years, I was aware of her presence and leadership in the community, especially at the college level.

Years later, Doc became a patient, oddly enough, in my pediatric department. She was quite ill and had been previously in the critical care nursing unit with congestive heart failure and internal bleeding. Even prior to this admission, she had been a patient in many other nursing units of the hospital.

But this time, when she was to be transferred from critical care to another unit, she announced, "I'll die before I go to that unit again."

She was told that the only other unit with empty beds was pediatrics. Pediatrics, at that time, was a combination of pediatric and medical/surgical beds, with pediatric beds on one end of the hall and adult beds on the other. Most adults admitted to this unit were young people, certainly not in their eighties, as Doc was. Nonetheless, Doc said, "That's where I will go." And in she came.

On hearing the news of her transfer to our unit, those of us who had previously had her as an anatomy professor were quite fearful, but Doc soon put us at ease. She enjoyed bragging about the fact that we were her students.

For some reason, she decided that she liked our unit. Upon subsequent admissions to the hospital, she always asked to be in our unit. Each admission created dread for the nursing staff, for she was usually seriously ill and needed much care and attention. There was always the fear that this could be the end, and no one wanted her to die on their shift.

Doc knew she was dying and requested that resuscitation mechanisms not be used. On one occasion she did quit breathing briefly. I was not there at the time, but another staff member stood by the bedside, holding her hand. After a few seconds, she began to breathe, opened her eyes, and asked what had happened. Surprisingly, she again recovered and was discharged to go home.

Over the next several years, we became very attached to Doc. I found it interesting to discover that in spite of her age and ill health she was always able to evaluate my staff and their performance. After I would return from a vacation or several days off duty, she would give me a full evaluation of the unit's activities. This would include who provided the best care, what made one nurse better than another, which nurses (including

133

students) showed the most potential, and who from the P.R.N. pool (nurses assigned to work in an area needing help for a given shift) she did not want to care for her again.

Doc always wanted to remain in control of her life and to be included in decisions about her care. This frequently created extra stress for the nurses and physicians, because her needs increased as she became more debilitated.

But in spite of her needs, I found my fears and dread changing to love. I occasionally had to reflect on those first student days and realize how our roles had reversed. It was strangely difficult to acknowledge that my fear had turned to love. By then, I was often in a position of control, in spite of her efforts not to let go.

Frequently I sat on the edge of her bed, held her hand or head, and listened as she cried or shared her frustrations and fears. As she approached her final days, I would sometimes hold her hand, and just say to her, "I love you" and she would whisper, "I know you do."

Seeing with New Eyes

By Lois Ann Ranck

Lois Ann Ranck lives in Mt. Joy, Pennsylvania. She served three years with Eastern Mennonite Board of Missions in Kenya, teaching community health workers and establishing an immunization clinic and mobile clinic in the bush. She currently workers in a pediatrics outpatient clinic with oncology, hematology, AIDS patients, and does well-child and acute care.

"Expect nothing but be prepared for anything." This is often the truth in day-to-day nursing anywhere, but it seemed even more so in the Maternal Child Health Clinic at Rhamu, Kenya.

All seemed to be going well. I was assisting a nurse in preparing immunization supplies for another busy day in the Maternal Child Health Clinic. The program was new, and the community people were bringing their children, newborns through five years, to the clinic. We were giving immunizations against the six childhood "killer diseases" of tuberculosis, diphtheria, tetanus, whooping cough, polio, and measles.

Teaching the mothers and caregivers about the diseases and how to prevent them was a necessary part of our work. Many mothers could relate stories of their children either suffering or dying from these diseases. Tuberculosis is still prevalent today. As recently as 1981, an outbreak of measles followed by

135

whooping cough took the lives of many children. Therefore the immunization program was well received. The people showed interest by their questions and concerns during home visits as well as by their regular attendance at the clinic.

Some injections caused minor side effects, such as fever and swollen areas. One February morning I was confronted by an upset mother named Isha and her one-and-a-half-year-old daughter, Fatuma. Isha refused to allow Fatuma to have the scheduled booster immunization because Fatuma's previous injections had made her unable to walk by herself. Though Fatuma had not been walking by herself previously, her mother thought she should be by now.

Fatuma was affectionate. As I picked her up, she put her frail arms quickly around my shoulders. However, this behavior seemed unusual. Most children scream the minute a stranger reaches out to them, especially in the immunization clinic.

Then I saw what appeared to be large gray clouds over both of Fatuma's pupils. She was indeed afraid to walk by herself when I put her on the floor. A finger or hand waved in front of her nose caused no blinking of her eyes. Several other health workers also checked her. We decided she was partially, if not completely, blind.

Fatuma's mother could see there was something wrong with her eyes. But much careful explanation was needed to convince her that the problem had probably existed since birth and was not associated with the immunizations.

Finally Isha agreed to have her daughter receive the booster injection. She also permitted her to see the eye doctor, who made a special flight to Rhamu every few months to assess eye problems in the area. Cataracts in elderly people are a common health problem. But the doctor confirmed that Fatuma, although a child, had cataracts in both eyes, most likely present since birth. He recommended special surgery in Nairobi, the largest city in Kenya and over 800 miles away.

I escorted Isha and Fatuma to Nairobi on a small plane. A special bond formed among the three of us. I tried to imagine myself as Isha, making my first trip from the bush to the city, totally dependent on others. Interestingly enough, the pronunciation of the mother's name, Isha, sounds the same as the word for eye in the Somali language.

Just as Isha was eyes for Fatuma, I was eyes for Isha in her first exposure to Nairobi. From the time we left Rhamu's airstrip until we arrived back three weeks later, I was the main source of Isha's communicable tongue, Somali, even though my vocabulary was limited.

Isha and Fatuma were admitted to the hospital, and the staff assisted Fatuma toward eyesight. Both cataracts were removed, and with the aid of strong glasses Fatuma began to discover a new world of dark and light, colors, and large objects. She would react with laughs, frowns, or blinks. She also started to walk without assistance. Fatuma's constant expression of happiness as she discovered and explored her new world of sight brought joy to us all.

Just as exciting was orienting Isha to the city. Going to town was a major event. She said the commotion of people and many vehicles was like the "shifting of goats and camels in the bush in search of water." Hot and cold running water, bathtubs, flush toilets, light switches, stairs, and dolls seemed magical to Isha compared with her simple Rhamu lifestyle. I had a hard time trying to explain that mannequins were not dead people, as she thought. Isha often told me that this experience was her new "eyesight"!

After being with Isha and Fatuma in the city, I read Numbers 10:29-31, where Moses wanted his father-in-law to be "eyes" for the people in the wilderness. Now I could understand in a new way how Isha felt in her "wilderness," a big, new city where she did not know the way.

I learned a lot from Isha and Fatuma as I worked closely with them. I saw Isha as a brave person, who took big risks and trusted people as she hoped for the best. I am grateful that Fatuma could be helped. As she gets older, she will need surgery again and frequent changes in her eyeglasses. But hope for her future remains bright.

Reprinted with permission from Missionary Messenger *and the author.*

The Patient Nurse

by Marie M. Leasa

Marie M. Leasa lives in Downington, Pennsylvania. She has worked as a staff nurse in intensive care and in pediatrics.

What do you do when the tables are turned and you are the patient instead of the nurse? After twenty years of nursing, it was difficult receiving care instead of giving it. In a period of six months, my life turned topsy-turvy.

August 12, 1988, was hot and muggy. I wore a sundress to my doctor's appointment. A week earlier, I'd had minor surgery—a biopsy on a lump that had suddenly appeared on the right side of my neck.

As I sat in the small exam room waiting to hear the results, I overheard the office staff conversing, and one word caught my attention—"malignancy." I had no idea who or what they were talking about, but I broke out in a sweat. My heart started to pound, and I considered "fight or flight," preferably flight.

My doctor entered the room. While closing the door he said, "Well, Marie, we have a problem."

A stab of horrible sinking panic grabbed me; I felt ill—as though I'd been kicked and beaten in the stomach. I heard little else the doctor said. All I knew was that I had cancer. The big "C" had hit me. Life—if I had any left—would never be the same.

That evening my oldest daughter, Jenny, made a birthday cake for her dad, who had turned forty that day. Somehow we got through the birthday dinner with all the relatives.

During the next few days and weeks, I received many cards and calls from friends and my family in California. They sent verses on the cards. Although I knew they were trying to help, sometimes those verses made me angry. I'm not sure just what I wanted to hear, but it wasn't Scripture.

I did realize that they loved me, but it was hard being 3,000 miles away from my parents, six sisters, and two brothers. What I really wanted was to be around my loud, crazy, emotional, Irish Catholic family. I wanted them to hug me and cry with me.

But the Lord had different ideas. I was stuck in Pennsylvania. Growing up in southern California and attending Catholic grammar school, high school, and college, I'd never heard of Mennonites until I met Varden. We've now been married almost twenty-one years and have lived in Pennsylvania the last fifteen. We attended Varden's parents' church, Frazer Mennonite, most of that time. I had finally been baptized as an adult and joined the Mennonite church in 1985. It was in this setting, not California, that the Lord planned to meet me with the support of church and family that I needed.

Over the next five months, I underwent more diagnostic tests, surgery, then twelve weeks of radiation therapy—the most difficult part of the ordeal. The radiation made me sick to my stomach several times a day (I lost twenty pounds). It took away my voice for a month, gave me a terribly sore throat (swallowing water felt like swallowing bits of broken glass), and sent me into the depths of depression.

I can remember sitting in church Sunday after Sunday looking at all the heads in front of me, wondering how this had happened to me and not some other person. I went up to the front on many Sundays during the caring-and-sharing time to ask for prayer, and my voice never wavered. But back in the pew, as I sang the hymns, my heart would break and the tears flowed freely.

> Teach me to feel that thou art always nigh;
> Teach me the struggles of the soul to bear;
> To check the rising doubt, the rebel sigh;
> Teach me the patience of unanswered prayer.
> —from the song "Spirit of God"

> Prayer is the burden of a sigh,
> The falling of a tear.
> —from the song "Prayer Is the Soul's Sincere Desire"

If that was the case, I did more praying in those months than ever before.

A second surgery involved removal of my spleen and multiple biopsies of lymph nodes to determine if and how far the cancer had spread. Afterward my mom, Mary Moy, came to help out at home for about two weeks. Each morning after breakfast we had Bible study, which helped me develop the habit of Bible meditation each day. Mom is also a registered nurse, and it was such a unique time—to have her all to myself. Giving me her love and care, she nurtured me physically, emotionally, and spiritually.

I'd never sat down and read the Bible at length—but as I did, slowly God became real and close to me. Especially comforting were the Psalms. I could tell that David and the other psalmists had experienced great suffering. Another reassuring Scripture I claimed was Isaiah 43. My father, Ken Moy, is an artist and carved a plaque with this verse for me:

> Don't be afraid for I have ransomed you. I have called you by name, you are mine. When you go through deep waters and great trouble, I will be with you. When you go through rivers of difficulty, you will not drown! When you walk through the fire of oppression, you will not be burned up—the flames will not consume you.

141

I am now back to work as a full-time, primary nurse in the pediatric/adolescent area of a small community hospital—Paoli Memorial. Since my illness, I see life in a different light. Things that used to upset me before seem less troubling. Before getting upset, I try to ask myself, "Is this really important? Is this really a problem?" If it is, I try to confront it calmly and deal with it, although I confess there are still some times when I just freak out at Varden, Jenny, or Adrienne. Anyone raising teenagers knows the challenge I'm talking about.

I pray more now—for myself, my husband, children, friends, family, co-workers, and my patients. I've found out firsthand just how powerful prayer is, and I use flash prayers frequently throughout the day. I also write down a verse or two that's meaningful or uplifting to me and take it to work each morning. It rests on top of my medication cart and reminds me during the day—especially when I'm stressed—to call on the Lord.

Since my illness, I've come in contact with more patients that need chemotherapy and/or radiation. At the appropriate time, I often share with them a little of my pilgrimage. I have felt a true communion of spirit with these individuals. So in a sense I feel the Lord has given me a special gift; I cherish that.

I've learned that it is a blessing to graciously receive as well as to give. I've learned that my spirit can soar with delight at simple glimpses of nature, such as the light from a crystal-clear full moon, or a blue jay perched on a forsythia branch.

I never would have requested this test, but it has refined me and taught me. I'm still in the process of learning from this whole experience. I can now, with the psalmist, ask God to bless me with life so I may continue to obey him (Ps. 119:17).

A Gentle Sensitivity

by A. Michael Nachtigall
as told to Janice Unruh Davidson

A. Michael Nachtigall lives in Newton, Kansas. He is a recent graduate of Bethel College (Kansas) and works as a staff nurse.

Janice Unruh Davidson lives in Valley Center, Kansas. She is director of nursing for Bethel College. She has worked in gerontology and psych nursing.

Historically nurses have been female, but the number of males joining the nursing profession is increasing. Frequently male nursing students are asked if they are going to be a *male* nurse.

Our response is typically, "No, I'm going to be a *nurse*."

Despite the frequent misunderstanding of their role, males have a great deal to contribute to the nursing profession and have already offered much to Christian nursing. Stories of caring from nurses who are female are plentiful, but males also have much caring to contribute. The following illustrates my experience as a nurse.

A patient in her early 40s was admitted to the orthopedic unit of a rural hospital for complications resulting from several previous bone fusions in her back. The patient was emotional and experiencing frequent muscle spasms and pain in her legs.

Nothing the nursing staff did seemed to help the patient, and the nurses didn't know what else to do. Because I had earlier developed a rapport with the patient, it was determined that I should be assigned to her when I arrived for the night shift.

By midnight, the patient had been increasingly complaining of leg cramping but had already received the prescribed pain medication. I contacted the doctor and another pain medication was provided, but the patient continued to be in distress.

To help settle her down, I went into the room to spend some time comforting her. Among her complications was a body cast which made rest uncomfortable. Propping the patient with pillows and soothing her in related ways had not worked.

Finally I began massaging her feet. Slowly she began to quiet down. After about thirty minutes of foot massage and gentle conversation, the patient said she felt she might be able to sleep.

I turned off the light and left the room. The patient slept soundly the rest of the night without needing further medication or intervention.

Here I Come, Feet First!

by Martha J. Rohrer

Martha J. Rohrer lives in Dayton, Virginia. She is a nurse midwife and has served several years in Pennsylvania and sixteen and a half years in Ethiopia.

After serving sixteen and a half years as a missionary nurse in Ethiopia, I decided to take midwifery education and become a certified nurse midwife. Daughters of my friends were asking me to assist them in home births since I had delivered so many babies when abroad. I felt this was a calling from God and have experienced God's guidance and wisdom in many situations that have occurred in the last ten years.

Trish was having her first baby and did not want to deliver in the hospital. I told her I preferred that first babies be born in the hospital. But she and her husband were both determined to deliver at home, so I consented to help them.

A prenatal check that bright June morning revealed that the baby was in a breech position and the presenting part was high. I hoped and prayed that it would turn to vertex in the next week, before her due date or before labor started.

But she called after six that evening to tell me her water broke when she was squatting. She was having a few mild contractions. Later instead of going to bed for the night I went to Trish.

145

I found her uncomfortable with labor but well in control and relaxed. However, she was eight centimeters dilated, and the baby was still presenting feet first. I suggested they go to the hospital, but they begged to stay home. Against my better judgment, I agreed. It was midnight.

One hour later Trish was fully dilated and ready to push. All went well until delivery of the head. I almost panicked! She pushed, her husband pushed on her abdomen, and I pulled. After what seemed a long time (but was probably only a few minutes), the head delivered. The baby was limp. I immediately did CPR and gave oxygen. The baby started to breathe and gave a good cry.

That cry was the sweetest music to my ears! The parents were praying and crying together. And I was crying and praising the Lord for answered prayer and the gift of life. That is a very special little girl to me even to this day. And you can be sure the next time I detected a baby preparing to come feet first I quickly sent the mother to the hospital.

Victory in Death

by Adella Kanagy

Adella Kanagy lives in Belleville, Pennsylvania. She has worked as a staff nurse, office nurse, and hospice chaplain. She served twenty-two years in Japan with Mennonite Board of Missions.

As a member of a home health care agency's hospice team, I made my first visit to Ida's home. I knew she was terminally ill with cancer. Her daughter opened the door, and I paused to learn from her a little about her mother's condition and care.

"I have to feed her, or she wouldn't eat," explained the daughter. "Someone else comes in to stay with her at night so that I can rest. The rest of the time I'm doing all her care. My husband would send her to the hospital, but I can't. She's the last of her family of five brothers and sisters."

Until she was eighty-five, Ida had kept her own neat apartment, attached to her daughter and son-in-law's home. During my visit, Ida explained that she had sold her own large home to move to her daughter's home two years earlier, after she was diagnosed with cancer.

"I'm so glad that they told me," she exclaimed, "so I could get ready." Then she explained about her husband's death fourteen years earlier and her son's death—with leukemia— more recently. Her manner reflected courage. Her radiant smile spoke of peace.

She said she was too tired to read the Bible for herself any longer. So I offered to read to her. She requested her favorite passage, Psalm 121.

> I lift up my eyes to the hills—where does my help come from? My help comes from the Lord, the Maker of heaven and earth. He will not let your foot slip—he who watches over you will not slumber. . . . He will watch over your life; the Lord will watch over your coming and going both now and forevermore.

From the window by her bed, Ida had lifted her eyes many times to view the wide, blue expanse of the Tuscarora Mountains. She had turned often for help to the Maker of those mountains. But this day when she heard the words, she reflected, "We don't really know what *forevermore* means, do we?"

On my next visit the following week, Ida told me, "I'm getting weaker; I'm waiting . . . when I have pain, sometimes I wonder if this will be it."

Her beautiful smile showed no fear as she thought of death, no complaints. I read to her Jesus' words that he is the bread of life and that the one who feeds on Jesus' bread will live forever.

Her thought for me that day was, "Everything we have is just loaned to us, isn't it?"

A week later was my last visit with her. Her daughter said her mother was no longer eating or drinking and hadn't recognized them for more than a day. "I need someone to tell me if what I'm doing is right," the distressed daughter said.

I sat with Ida while her daughter and son-in-law were in another room. Her eyes were half open, but she gave no response. Her shallow breathing, weak pulse, and open, mute mouth were signs of her passing from the life that had been loaned to her. With my hand on her forehead, or holding her cool hand, I read Psalms and prayed again for the Lord's care for her now and forevermore.

After an hour at her bedside I met her daughter again as I

left. I assured her that her care of her mother was a special gift as the end of her mother's journey approached. All she needed now was tender loving care and her daughter's presence.

That night at midnight Ida's journey on this earth ended. Her daughter, son-in-law, and home health nurse were at her side. Now Ida knows more fully what *forevermore* means. Because of her faith in Christ, death was a victory for her.

Volunteer Nursing

by Pearl Zehr

Pearl Zehr lives in New Wilmington, Pennsylvania. She has worked with refugees in Malaysia. She has also worked as a pediatric office nurse, staff nurse for medical—nursing, and as a nursing educator.

Nursing has been my profession for thirty-seven years. Last year I had my first opportunity to do extended volunteer nursing for refugees living in Sungai Besi Transit Camp for Vietnamese Boat People, located near Kuala Lumpur, Malaysia.

The camp contained about 6,000 persons ranging in age from birth to about seventy years, with the average age being twenty to thirty years. I was privileged to hand out materials prepared in the western hemisphere to express love and care for these men, women, and children. We distributed toiletry kits to family members who accompanied patients needing consultation and treatment at the nearby hospital in Kuala Lumpur.

Early each morning our health care team from World Concern met for a half-hour prayer time. Then it was morning rounds for the patients admitted to sick bay, after which we saw patients in the clinic until lunchtime. We saw ninety to a hundred patients per day during morning and afternoon clinic hours, with English-speaking Vietnamese refugees acting as interpreters.

After lunch and before afternoon clinic hours we performed EKG's, made solutions for washing wounds (abscesses, impetigo lesions, and so forth), and sterilized surgical instruments. Refugee staff workers prepared cotton balls and cut and folded dressings from a large gauze roll to save money.

There were no Hollister bags for the colostomy of the child with Hirschsprung's disease. But we did have Destrostixs for the diabetics. And we had adequate antibiotics for staph and streptococcal infections, pneumonias, and fevers. Plenty of oral rehydration salts were available for the gastroenteritis patients. We could also help alleviate abdominal distress and soreness from parasites with the three-day treatment of Mebendazole.

Children under five could have milk to drink twice a day. Those who were underweight could come to the child health clinic for vitamins. Every day we handed out malaria pills to complete the patient's fourteen days of treatment.

Several Vietnamese refugee doctors and two midwives staffed the camp on evenings, nights, and weekends. I had been volunteering at the camp for six months before a second doctor was hired to assist in the health program.

My rewards in volunteering came in experiencing the love and graciousness of these Vietnamese people. They showed their appreciation with words and deeds of kindness to each other and to the staff. Even the children's eyes sparkled as they gestured their thank you's. Some of my new friends are now settling in the U.S. and Canada. With several just across the border in Canada, I now have telephone and letter contact.

I pray that in their new homes these refugees may find salt-and-light Christians who will share with them the hope and purpose we have in Christ.

A Foot Washing Service

by Christine Holsopple Kauffman

Christine Holsopple Kauffman lives in Goshen, Indiana. She served five years with Mennonite Central Committee in Guatemala. She has done home health care and pediatric emergency room nursing.

The phone rang about 6:00 a.m. It was Tomas to tell us that Matilda had gone into labor about 8:00 the night before. Just before dawn she had left her position by her fire in her hut and walked the two and a half hours up the steep Guatemalan hill to the closest car-traveled road.

We went to pick her up with our small four-wheel-drive vehicle. When we got to her, she was having hard contractions, about five minutes apart. This was Matilda's third pregnancy. Her first pregnancy produced a cute little girl, now four years old.

Her second pregnancy brought a labor and delivery that was difficult. The baby was in a breech position. Tomas thought his wife was going to die through the process. The baby did die.

Now in her third pregnancy, labor had begun. The baby was in a breech position again. I had been doing frequent prenatal checks and urged her to stay close to town, where the hospital was located. For several weeks Matilda stayed close to town. But being in town was much different than being out in the village where she could make her own tortillas and where fire-wood was easily accessible. For these reasons, Matilda decided to return to her village, even though she knew she was farther from hospital care.

Now the time had come for delivery. She had made a great effort to get to a health facility, and I wanted to help her with the process.

The hospital was operated by the Spanish—the elite of the country. The staff did not know Matilda's indigenous language. I did as much interpreting as possible. But once she went into the labor room, I was not allowed to be with her. Thinking that the medical staff would do a c-section soon, I ran some errands and returned.

Tomas and I waited and waited. I finally insisted that I see Matilda and talk to the nurses and doctors. The report was that labor was progressing slowly because the patient was not re-laxed. Later I discovered that the real problem was that, al-though she was experiencing a lot of pain, her uterus was not functioning normally.

At midnight after Matilda had some fainting spells and the baby's heart rate was decreasing, the doctors decided on a c-section. In answer to our prayer, she delivered a healthy boy.

The next afternoon, I visited Matilda and the baby, almost forty-eight hours after she had left her home. Her first request was that I help her to the bathroom. Again, because the hospi-tal staff was all Spanish, little attention was given to the Kekchi mothers.

In the bathroom I glanced down. My eyes caught her feet and sandals. Still caked with mud from the long walk in from her village, they now also had blood streaks from her recent de-livery procedure.

I was caught off guard, and Matilda noticed my prolonged glance. I could not believe that the nurses or someone had not cared enough to give her a bath.

"Would you wash my feet and legs?" she asked timidly. I did.

When I finished Matilda said in her quiet way, *"Bantiox hermana* (thank you sister)."

There had been no white basin with a clean white towel. There were no neatly trimmed toenails or clean feet to wash. I had never been in a "service" quite like this before. But it was the most meaningful foot washing I have ever experienced.

Lamaze for the Amish

by Nadene Brunk

*Nadene Brunk lives in Bridgewater, Virginia. She has been a
Lamaze instructor for several years and teaches maternal child
nursing. She has also done home health.*

Many Amish have bought farms around my parental home in
another state. One summer my mother knew eight Amish
women who lived nearby were pregnant. She wanted them to
have a Lamaze childbirth class.

Knowing I was a Lamaze teacher, she called me up and said,
"Next time you visit, bring all your stuff. I'll have a night where I
invite all of them and their husbands. I don't know if they will
come, but you come prepared."

I went with my charts, but I was scared! I was scared mostly
because my parents would be there. I use words in Lamaze
class that I have never said in front of my parents before. I got
out my charts and wasn't even sure I wanted my mother to see
them, let alone some Amish women. There were all kinds of
pictures!

I didn't know how to dress or how to act. How could I teach
in one night what I usually teach in six classes? Mother said she
had heard the Amish women talk, and they often expressed
fear of their labor and delivery experience. Mother hoped my
instruction would make these pregnancies more positive.

Half an hour before they all came, I got up the nerve to show the charts and pictures to my mother. "Do you think they will be offended by this one, or this one?"

She was no help. She kept saying, "Well, I don't know. I just don't know!" I think she was a little amazed herself. So I decided I'd have to wing it.

Wouldn't you know it, all eight of the Amish women came *with* their husbands. I am sure they came partly because they also felt comfortable in my parents' home, where they often came to use the kitchen phone. My mother has also taken Amish woman who are in labor to the hospital.

As they arrived, I knew that they all knew each other, but they would not speak to one another. They just sat down and stared at me. Finally I launched into my presentation, essentially just reviewing the basics of childbirth and delivery. They asked no questions. They seemed neither impressed nor stunned by anything I showed them. They just sat there.

When I finished, my father spoke up. "Do you think it is good for the men to be there when their wives have babies?"

That of course was a big question. I answered, "Well, my husband felt it was very valuable and I have heard many fathers talk about it. Some have said it was a life-changing experience for them. They've said it has been so much easier for them to feel like the baby was their child. It wasn't just *her* child but *theirs*. It made a difference in the type of care they gave. I think it has profound effects on fathers."

Then my dad said, almost with tears in his eyes, "I really feel like I missed something."

That statement meant a lot to me. It was his way of approving what I was doing.

Then Mother served strawberry cake and ice cream. The women all went to the kitchen and the men stayed in the living room with Dad. *That* was when the women started asking questions, things they wouldn't mention around the men.

After that experience I wanted to go back and be a midwife in the area or set up a shop in my mother's home. They were so hungry to know more.

It was a gift my mother gave me, without realizing it. It was also a gift to herself. I think she always wondered what I did in Lamaze childbirth classes!

New Life

by Joy Reichenbach

Joy Reichenbach lives in Bluffton, Ohio. She has worked as a staff nurse and in staff development and nursing administration in gerontology.

It would be miraculous to have a dying patient suddenly sit up, open his or her eyes, and be totally well. But what a miracle it has been to watch dying patients be set free from this world to go to a place where there are no tears, sorrow, or pain. Where they can indeed get up and be totally well.

I remember a woman who struggled with severe emphysema. She was having a difficult time breathing and was in severe pain. We did what we could with medication and oxygen to keep her comfortable. Still she suffered. Another nurse and I stayed with her, lifting her up and laying her down at her request as she gasped for air.

We spoke briefly of the future, of her desire to be free from this life, and of her longing to find peace in a heavenly place. We held hands—hers cool and perspiring. My arms tired from supporting her head and upper body. She also would seem to tire and needed to lie back down, only to need air again and come back up.

We worked together, all the time silently praying for God's miracle. Then finally she was quiet. After a few minutes the miracle happened: she peacefully left this world. In that moment it was as if I should start singing the "Hallelujah Chorus." I wanted to clap for her and shout, "Congratulations! Enjoy life again in a new and better way!"

That experience, along with others in which I stayed by the side of dying persons, gives me a broader perspective to live by. Life is more valuable as I have seen the assurance and courage of those who experience death.

Death is also easier to accept. It is more than the end of life. It is the beginning of a new and improved life. As Paul said, "When the perishable has been clothed with the imperishable, and the mortal with immortality, then the saying that is written will come true: 'Death has been swallowed up in victory'" (1 Cor. 15:54).

Nursing has done me a favor and helped guide my life as I have experienced the life and death of the people I have cared for.

My Coach

by Josephine Banks

Josephine Banks and Barbara Beiler live in San Antonio, Texas. Josephine is not a nurse but wrote as a tribute to and in exchange for the services of nurse midwife Barbara. Barbara served in Belize under Eastern Mennonite Board of Missions.

It was the tenth hour of labor. The baby had not dropped and my cervix was not dilating as much as Barbara Beiler, my certified nurse-midwife, would have liked. I am not a nurse. This was my first pregnancy, and I had no confidence that I could make it through childbirth.

With each contraction I started to cry in distress, "I can't do this."

Barbara held my hand tightly and said confidently, "You're doing it, Mamma."

"Is the baby going to be all right?" questioned my mother, who was substituting for my husband.

"She's going into transition. It won't be long," Barbara comforted her. My mother had never experienced a labor, not even her own, because she was medicated during the births of my brother and me. She searched Barbara's face for signs of concern. But Barbara's calmness gave her some peace.

Barbara looked straight into my eyes. "Jo Anne, you've done a terrific job so far. Do you feel like pushing yet?"

I nodded. "Every time I get a contraction."

"Are you ready to have this baby?"

A contraction interrupted my answer.

"Will you help your daughter?" Barbara asked my mother, while motioning her to sit on the bed and hold my legs so that she might help me push.

"I'm scared I can't do this!" I tried to bolt out of bed.

"You're doing this, Mamma," Barbara gently urged me back onto the bed.

"Can we say a prayer?" I asked.

Barbara, my mother, and I bowed our heads and prayed for a safe delivery. The room grew calm, even though the situation was critical. For an hour I pushed. But my mother grew petrified when she saw that I no longer had any energy left to give.

"Here, Mamma, do you want to feel your baby?" Barbara took my hand and held it so that I could feel the baby's head.

"Are we almost there? I can't do this anymore!" I moaned.

"But you're doing it, Mamma," Barbara assured me.

My mother looked with amazement at Barbara, who remained calm even though it seemed the second stage was moving slowly.

Then Barbara commanded, "Push! One, two, three, four, five, six. . . ." Barbara and my mother held me up to a sitting position so that I could push the baby out. Barbara's voice continued to help guide my pushing, ". . . seven, eight, nine."

Today my mother says she will never forget the sight of her grandchild slipping out and landing in Barbara's welcoming hands. I remember watching Barbara quickly make sure the baby was all right. And then I heard the words I never expected to hear, "You did it, Mamma."

The baby was placed on my abdomen. All three of us forgot the past moment's anxiety. We basked in the magic and energy that my son, Roger, had brought with him to begin his new life.

Short Anecdotes

When I was working as a rehabilitation nurse for residents in a nursing home, I met a nineteen-year-old man with muscular dystrophy who had had a stroke. He was unable to move his legs or his right arm and unable to talk.

I worked with him for two years and he gradually learned to communicate some again with the help of a speech therapist. I discovered he used to go fishing and asked him if he would like to go. With a little encouragement, he said yes, and we went! He eventually started drawing again with his left hand, and some of his pictures were sold.

When I left the facility, I kept in touch with him for the next several years. One night I was called because he was in heart failure and near death. I visited him for about two hours. He knew he was dying and we talked about that. He had no fear of death.

He wanted to give me something, something I had always admired. It was a poster that he kept above his bed. On it was a single red rose on a black background. The rose had one petal that had fallen from it to the table below. The caption on the picture said, "Is it any less a rose?"

He died about an hour after I left. I think about that picture a lot. It reminds me that just because someone has lost function doesn't mean he or she is any less a person.

—*Velda Garber-Weider, Harrisonburg, Virginia*

One New Year's Eve the emergency room called and said a man was being transferred up because he whistled when he coughed. We discovered that he had aspirated a noisemaker into his trachea and needed to have it fiberoptically removed.

—Esther White, Hesston, Kansas

One patient always had trouble remembering my last name, *Horst.* So I told her to just think of a horse and put a *t* on the end. The next day I asked her if she could remember my name. She thought for a moment and said, "Why yes. It's Mrs. Pig."

—Ida Horst, Newton Medical Center, Newton, Kansas

In my early years, a brochure from Toronto Sick Children's Hospital arrived in our home. The picture of a large graduating class of immaculately uniformed nurses caught my eye. The accompanying information gave the address to which further questions and applications could be directed. I hid this away for a while, then decided to write. They would not know I was only nine or ten. Needless to say my mother was shocked when a reply came addressed to me—so there was a little inquest.

Several years later—I was twenty-one and raising ducks in the summer to earn my way, I was accepted for nursing education at the Kitchener-Waterloo Hospital.

In those days, the Superintendent of Nursing gave the applicant the address for ordering uniform and apron material and instructions for design. We waited anxiously for the material one week before I reported for class, the parcel arrived.

My mother and a kindly neighbor worked feverishly to complete three blue and white striped uniforms, six aprons and bibs, three stiff collars, and six pairs of cuffs. Each outfit required approximately thirty-five buttons as all was held together with studs which needed two buttonholes! This totaled over seventy holes and our treadle sewing machine didn't make them! But they all got done thanks to my dear mother and a neighbor.

—Edna Hunsperger Bowman, Cambridge, Ontario

Over the years I have cared for many patients who had trouble voiding, for one reason or another. I could never understand quite why. I thought that if they could only relax, everything would be okay. Then I had surgery. When the catheter came out, I couldn't void either. The problem continued for nearly two weeks, with the catheter in and out numerous times.

Then I got the idea that if I could just go home, everything would be okay. I lived across a ravine and on top of a small but steep hill behind the La Junta hospital. Finally the doctor let me try. I crossed the ravine and climbed the hill. Sure enough, it worked!

—Alice Martin, Hesston, Kansas

One Christmas eve when I was working as the supervisor of a nursing home, I coaxed my husband to come to the home dressed as Santa Claus.

But when he walked into one room where there were some disoriented patients, one of them said, "Oh my goodness! I didn't believe it would end like this!"

—Janice Unruh Davidson, Hesston, Kansas

When I was in nursing school, one of my classmates was caring for a cardiac patient by helping with a tub bath. He was in the bathroom a long time.

When she knocked to see if he was okay, he said, "I'm just trying to figure out how to wear these pajamas."

Then she realized that she had given him a laundry bag instead of a pair of pajamas.

—Lois Stolifer, Hesston, Kansas

After only four months of Mandarin Chinese language study at the Mennonite Christian Hospital in Taiwan, I was reassured hearing this story about Gladys Siebert, who spent twenty-five years in Taiwan at MCH.

One day when a patient died and the family came, Gladys broke the news gently to them that the patient's body had been put in the morgue.

Judging from their startled response, she realized she had used the correct words but the wrong tones. What she had actually told them was that the body had been put in the Pacific Ocean!

—*Dianna Eshleman, Hualien, Taiwan*

Our vehicle was grinding slowly through the sandy trail in the jungle of the Paraguayan Chaco. We were a team of a doctor, nurses, and a secretary on a public health mission. A campaign had been announced against tuberculosis, polio, eye disease, and goiter. Five thousand settlers in the many villages settled by Mennonites had been informed of our coming and exhorted for total participation. We made periodic trips to accommodate the many settlers living in far out villages, some up to 120 kilometers from the central hospital.

Suddenly a group of horsemen came from seemingly nowhere out of the bush and stopped our vehicle. What did they want? We were not used to holdups here in this forlorn jungle.

But no, these were not pirates. They were cowboys working with cattle. They could not make it to the village so they asked for their check-up and vaccinations here on the road. They lifted their dirty, sweaty sleeves for the disinfection and injection, opened their dusty collars for the goiter check, and had their eyes examined. Smilingly we obliged and were happy they took this campaign seriously.

—*Freida Siemens Kaethler, Chaco, Paraguay*

The three women from Evergreen Hall—our Alzheimer's unit—were sitting at a round table in the day room. Dolly had little intact memory but still retained her social graces. She frequently asked other residents, visitors, or staff how they were doing today, or if they were tired. Then she'd politely wait for a response.

This particular afternoon Dolly turned to her neighbor, Esther, and stated in her most cheerful voice, "I knew you when you were still living."

Esther looked down at her body with amazement and shock, turned to Dolly, and challenged her in an irritated voice, "I thought I was still alive!"

Dolly made no response. She just calmly looked out the window. Marguerite listened to the exchange and comforted Esther with, "Well, you don't look dead to me."

After a slight pause, Dolly asked if they were tired, and the polite nonconversation continued. Only the nurse remembered, and smiled.

—*Mary L. Weaver*

In the 1930s, La Junta Hospital in Colorado had many patients with tuberculosis. One day a student nurse was interviewing a new patient and asked, "Do you cough?"

He replied, "Yes."

The nurse then asked, "Well, do you raise anything?"

He said, "Oh, yes, the finest potatoes in the county!"

—The Nightingale, *the La Junta Yearbook*

A vehicle was essential to serve the 250 residents in the native village in northern Canada where I was the community nurse. However the old red pickup had seen better days. The door wouldn't stay closed, requiring me to hang on tight when bouncing around corners on the rough roads. But starting the engine was the real challenge. "Always stop it on a slope or leave the motor running," I was advised.

Now it was dusk, two weeks into my assignment. I'd gone to the clinic to pick up supplies, but when I came out, the silence was disturbing. The engine had died. *Lord, you brought me here. You'll just have to see me through.*

Just then two men came walking down the road. After greeting them I asked if they would assist me with a little push. They responded with eager smiles. With thanks and a wave, I rejoiced on my way down the road to home, thanking and praising God for seeing me through.

—*Marianne Schlegal, Northern Alberta, Canada*

Many things happen during the night. Babies are born, death comes during sleep, accidents happen, and abuse and crime seem to be covered by the cloak of darkness.

One night I was awakened at 3:30 a.m. to come and see a person who had been shot in the small village in northern Alberta where I served as community nurse.

On arriving at the house which was overflowing with people, I was told, "Out behind the house."

Bravely I walked back carrying my constant companion, the black leather medical bag containing many things—including narcotics. There in the shadows of the almost full moon lay a man on his back, arms outstretched, gun close at hand. Was he shot, or was I being set up for a robbery?

Then I saw the wound in his chest. After examining him, I turned to the family members standing near, "Get a blanket and cover him. He's dead. The body should remain untouched until police come and give further instructions."

On covering the body, I realized that I had seen this man only days before. *God, he is in your hands,* I prayed.

—*Marianne Schlegal, northern Alberta, Canada*

He was old, but not acutely ill. As I made my rounds early one morning, he asked if I would call his daughter.

"Sure, but do you realize it's only 5:00 a.m.?"

His kind face smiled as he said, "That's okay; she won't mind."

So I called, and she didn't mind. "He seems just the same," I said, "but he asked me to call you."

Cheerfully, she said she'd be along soon. The next night when I came on duty, I learned that he'd died that day—but not before his daughter had come to see him.

—Clara Jutzi, Kitchener, Ontario

Johnny had no "book learning," but he was friendly and helpful to everyone as our hospital custodian in St. Anthony, northern Newfoundland. After years of faithful service, the aging process made him a patient in the hospital that had almost been his home. He asked to have all his friends come to see him, one by one.

When my turn came, he took my hand and with great poise said, "My time has come, and I wanted to thank you and tell you good-bye."

When he had spoken to everyone in this fashion, he left us. He may not have been a scholar or an orator, but Johnny knew about dying with dignity.

—Anna E. Wideman, Kitchener, Ontario

It required the pilot's experienced eyes to spot the small gray cluster of fishing shacks clinging to the rocks along that rugged Labrador coast. We swooped down. Moments after our pontoons sliced off the top of the waves, we settled to a rough roll.

A small fishing boat nosed its way around a giant, grimy iceberg that had grounded itself in the little cove. When we met, bobbing like two out-of-step dancers in that choppy sea, a mother handed over her eight-month-old baby girl, seriously ill with pneumonia.

I was a total stranger, but she'd already lost several babies to that harsh climate. The tears should have been hers instead of mine as the plane lifted. But she was rewarded for her calm trust. Recovered and healthy, baby Louisa did return to her mother's waiting arms.

—*Anna E. Wideman, Kitchener, Ontario*

Sixteen-year-old Jessica was transferred to my unit in the hospital from maternity, because she wanted to give her baby up for adoption. Although Jessica lived at home and was still in school, she never told her parents about her pregnancy. They thought that she was at her sister's apartment for the weekend, when actually she had come to the hospital and given birth to a baby.

Jessica worked part time at McDonald's after school and was planning to pay her own hospitalization fees, since she felt that she could not ask her parents for help.

But even though she had made her plans carefully, one aspect was overlooked. Jessica was too young to sign the legal papers for adoption. After discussing the situation in a joint meeting with the adoption agency, a social worker, her physician, and her older sister, Jessica was informed she had no alternative. Her parents would need to know about the baby.

I found Jessica sitting on the side of her bed with a heavy heart. She told me that her parents would disown her if they found out about this. I sat down by her side and put my arm around her while she sobbed.

A couple days after she was discharged from the hospital, a local florist came to my unit and handed me a single, long-stemmed red rose. My eyes filled with tears as I read the note. "Everything is fine with me and my family. Thanks again for your support and your dearest help. Love always, Jessica."

—*Erma Metzler, Manheim, Pennsylvania*

One day a ten-year-old girl was brought by her disabled father and siblings to the Clinica Luzy Esperanza (Light and Hope Clinic) in east Paraguay. She was in a coma and her back was profoundly arched. A spinal puncture confirmed a severe case of spinal meningitis. We admitted her to isolation and started the most aggressive treatment we could give at a small rural clinic.

Days passed, the fever lowered, but the coma continued. Even though we kept our costs at a minimum, the expense was draining the family's limited resources. Finally in desperation they made arrangements to take the child home—come what may. It was a sad choice, but we could not promise that she would wake up if she stayed at the clinic.

Then suddenly, on the morning of the tenth day, we noticed Maria's eyes following our movements. In the afternoon of that same day a favorite brother, Pedro, walked in. With joy she uttered the first syllable of his name. There was hardly a dry eye in the ward!

After that the improvement was progressively rapid. The family no longer looked at the expense as too draining, so she stayed on another five days until the feeding tubes were out and she had begun to feed herself. She then went home with an expected full recovery.

—*Sara V. Miller, Kalona, Iowa*

One rainy evening in rural Paraguay, a thirteen-year-old girl received a serious snake bite. Her father put her on the back of his motorcycle and set off for the Clinica Luzy Esperanza. They did not arrive until 2:00 a.m. the next morning—six hours after the bite—because he had to push the motorcycle through the mud all the way except for a brief stretch of hardtop.

The leg was swollen to the knee. Unhappily, there was no doctor here to call, only the Great Physician, and we sure did call on him. I started the antivenom treatment, including IV and antibiotics.

Sometime later we noticed tetanus setting in, and my assistant and I kept a bedside vigil in prayer that convulsions would not follow. Gradually the girl became quiet, the crisis passed, and she went on to make a good recovery.

As so often in our work we were aware that God does the healing not because of but in spite of who we are. Especially in our maternity work throughout the years we have often found ourselves at a disadvantage because of bad roads and no medical help available at short notice. But we always have prayer.

—*Sara V. Miller, Kalona, Iowa*

When the nursing school at Mennonite Christian Hospital in Hualien, Taiwan, began some thirty years ago, it was a stark two-story building. There were dorm rooms for students on the first floor and an empty shell on the second floor, waiting to become classrooms.

We had no nursing textbooks in Chinese but fortunately I had brought a set of new, updated nursing books from North America. It was a formidable task, but our best option was to summarize the texts into notes, then translate these notes into Chinese. I spent each evening summarizing and the next morning a Chinese translator/teacher would spend two to three hours with me putting the notes into Chinese.

Then we would "stencil" them via a ditto machine. Usually that afternoon I would teach the material to the students. Tedious, but effective. The total process of translating the core curriculum took about five years.

—*Susan Kehler, Sumas, Washington*

While viewing an exhibit at the Art Institute of Chicago one hot summer afternoon, I observed a teenage boy suddenly fall to the floor. As a critical care nurse, I immediately assessed the teenager and concluded that he had simply fainted as manifested by his strong pulse and adequate respirations.

Suddenly out of the crowd, a woman forcibly pushed a bewildered looking man forward shouting, "My husband's a doctor!"

As the doctor stooped down, looking back and forth from me to the unconscious teenager, he sheepishly said, "Actually, I am a dentist."

—Peggy Rupp Wysong, Goshen, Indiana

The room was abuzz when I walked in for postconference. Some students on one unit had witnessed their first resuscitation code and were excitedly telling the others about it. The other half of the group listened and asked questions. One student from Lebanon was perplexed. She had not seen as many TV shows and movies and had trouble understanding what happened.

As the room quieted down the students asked me what other codes the hospital had.

"Code green" I explained, "is a tornado watch. Code black is a tornado warning. We have still another code for a community disaster, for example if there were a bus accident or a manufacturing plant explosion. Perhaps you have heard of the Palm Sunday tornadoes, the day three tornadoes touched down in this town in the 1960s. That was a community disaster."

By then I was warmed up to the subject and kept on. "I have friends who were working in the emergency department that day. They tell horrible stories of victims and even of people carrying bushel baskets of arms and legs."

At that point the student from Lebanon interrupted, her face lit up. "Oh those! We have those all the time! You know! Bombings in Lebanon! People losing arms and legs! Now I know what you are talking about!"

We all grew silent and pondered the difference in her world and ours.

—Beth Landis, Goshen, Indiana.

Many years ago I was working in Paraguay as a nurse. One day when our physician was gone, a fifteen-year-old girl came with diabetes and without insulin. All we had was some outdated insulin, and we were ten days away from Asunción, the only source for more.

Finally another worker called a military station and arranged for a plane to parachute some to us. Neti was going into a diabetic coma when we got a message to put out a sheet to mark our location. Toward evening we heard a plane, and how we prayed that the pilot would see the sheet, but the sound disappeared and no insulin.

By morning, Neti was deep in a coma. Then a plane appeared in the sky and a parachute came drifting down with the precious medicine. By God's grace, Neti responded. And in appreciation, she became one of the most dedicated nurses at our leprosy clinic.

—*Clara R. Schmidt, Asunción, Paraguay*

Eighteen years ago when I was a camp nurse, a nine-year-old girl kept coming in for what I determined was just a little extra attention. She finally shared with me that her parents were in the middle of a divorce; she had no idea who she belonged to or where she belonged.

At the end of camp, she put her arms around me and said she didn't want to go home. We talked about the need to go back and deal with her parents and their situation. It was a tough assignment.

A few months ago, as I was teaching a Lamaze class, I found my eyes wandering to a beautiful young woman. She seemed close to her husband, as noted by touch and glances.

At break time she asked me, "Do you know who I am?"

She had seemed familiar, but I had to admit that I didn't recognize her.

"Don't you remember eighteen years ago, a little girl who spent a lot of time with you at camp?"

Immediately I knew! Over the next several weeks I got to know a radiant and grateful woman who now had a wonderful family situation.

—*Velda Garber-Weider, Harrisonburg, Virginia*

As a student, I was caring for a patient who was having a liver biopsy done. My teacher was also present during the procedure, simply *being with* the conscious patient—holding her hand and talking with her through the scary and painful ordeal.

When the physician asked my teacher to assist him, I was shocked that she refused, saying her job at that moment was to be with the patient. He would have to get somebody else to help him. That made a profound impression on me, suddenly communicating what nursing was all about.

—*Beryl Brubaker, Harrisonburg, Virginia*

Epilogue

by Janis Miller

Nursing is an evolving discipline. In the 1970s and into the '90s, we were looking at a process of defining our discipline. Perhaps more than anything, we attempted to answer the often-asked question: "Why don't you just go to medical school?"

The answer is partly that nursing defies strict classification as a discipline steeped only in the sciences. Seeing nursing as fundamentally caring is now a strong premise among nurses and throughout educational curriculums. Nursing views people as more than physical parts that merely need to be defined to understand the whole person.

Nursing is interested in human beings as unique and complex, as greater than the sum of their parts. And health is viewed not just as the correct mechanical workings of the stomach, lungs, and liver, but as a spiritual, social, emotional, and physical well-being.

Consequently, care for patients is time-intensive and includes family and other broad-reaching social, spiritual, and emotional support structures. It requires the nurse to develop that intuitive understanding which is now being talked about as the *art* of nursing.

Hidden between the lines of the stories in this book, there is the steady foundation of medical science. The stories demonstrate decisions made through critical thinking, logical gathering and processing of information, and structured planning and evaluating of care.

But the true focus of the book—the stories of nurses—has largely revealed the art of nursing. It is the less-well-defined but all-important exchange that occurs within a nurse-patient relationship. Perhaps it is this, more than any other reason, that maintains nurses' love of their discipline itself, and our sometimes heated defense of its unique focus.

A Historical Overview of Mennonite Nurses Association
(1942-1992)

It may seem ironic that an organization which focuses on healing and wholeness had its beginnings in cemeteries, but nurses are known for ingenuity and flexibility. In the late 1930s, travel time and finances were limited, so Mennonite nurses traditionally met between sessions of the Mennonite Board of Missions' (MBM) annual meeting. Not wanting to miss any sessions, and with limited indoor space, about two dozen nurses began to share their ideas in the cool and quietness of the cemetery of whatever congregation hosted that year's MBM annual meeting.

It was at such an event in Michigan that Maude Swartzendruber, supervisor of an MBM-sponsored tuberculin hospital in La Junta, Colorado, spoke to Verna Zimmerman, a recent nursing graduate from Lancaster, Pennsylvania. Maude shared her vision for a Mennonite nurses organization. The idea took root.

When Verna became a staff nurse at the La Junta hospital, Maude and she had more time to dream. Verna, with no copier and at her own expense (on a salary of $35 per month), sent cards to all Mennonite ministers and bishops asking for addresses of any Mennonite nurses they knew. Later she wrote to the nurses and suggested they meet at the next conference.

The result was gratifying. At the 1940 Hutchinson, Kansas, MBM meeting, Verna and Maude were appointed to organize a nursing association. They wrote a constitution but had no constituency. By June of 1942, the constitution was presented. Each nurse was asked to pay an annual $1 membership fee and the Mennonite Nurses Association was officially born.

One special concern which brought the nurses together was a need to foster Christian commitment and vision for service. These were war years, and some nurses were pondering the noncombatant WAC program. To encourage dialogue on this and communicate about other concerns, the first issue of *Mennonursing* later renamed *The Christian Nurse* was published in March 1945.

An early issue carried H. S. Bender's speech to the Pennsylvania nurses, "Can a Nonresistant Nurse Serve in the Army?" In it he suggested that if noncombatant roles in the military were inappropriate for men who felt war was wrong, the same was true for women.

The eight-page bimonthly publication was sent to anyone who requested it. There were no subscription fees. Three editors, Maude, Verna, and Ellen Coffman of Vineland, Ontario, each wrote a short editorial. Each issue had a list of nurses in "full-time service" and reports from nurses overseas.

Other nurses soon gave leadership to MNA, the newsletter, and their local chapters. The Harrisonburg, Virginia, chapter and Lancaster, Pennsylvania, chapter organized almost simultaneously with MNA. Gradually sixteen chapters developed.

The first project was in response to an appeal from Paraguay to raise $300 for the educating of a student nurse. Over $700 was contributed, which supported two student nurses. Each local group was encouraged to have a project. In 1945, there were six nurses in "mission work" and fourteen in "relief work." By 1962, there were thirty-nine missionary nurses and ten in relief work.

In the 1950s Mennonite nurses were earning degrees, and Mennonite schools of nursing had been started. In 1956, "as a courtesy," nurses were permitted a public evening program at the annual MBM meeting. Their presentation was well received and did much to raise respect for the professional quality of their service.

Practical nurses were included in MNA in 1955. By 1962, there were 704 members, including 124 students. Local chapters were autonomous in their structure and most met quarterly. Projects ranged from sending liver extract to Italy, handmade bibs and aprons to Israel, and money to India and Paraguay.

By 1970, MNA adopted a new structure with less organizational complexities. Local groups functioned more autonomously. MNA began meeting simultaneously with the Mennonite Medical Association, holding combined plenary sessions but separate business meetings.

Currently the association provides two $500 scholarships annually to deserving students at Mennonite colleges. Projects continue with approximately $2000 per year to such varied causes as healthy baby kits in Bolivia, wells in Haiti, textbooks for students in Uganda, and infant scales in El Salvador. Since 1973, a Nurse of the Year has been recognized annually.

Today numerous nursing associations exist, have newsletters, and hold conferences. But a closer look reveals that most of them are only five to twenty years old. Maude Swartzendruber and Verna Zimmerman were truly pioneers in their vision for MNA.

—Frances Bontrager Greaser
Goshen, Indiana

The Editors

Dave and Neta Jackson are full-time writers and editors who specialize in coauthoring books with others. They are the parents of two children, Julian (1969) and Rachel (1975). They have been members of Reba Place Fellowship in Evanston, Illinois, since 1973.

Dave was born in Glendale, California, the son of parents involved in rural church planting. He graduated from Multnomah School of the Bible, then from Judson College with a degree in journalism. He did graduate work in communications at Wheaton College. For eight years Dave was a pastoral elder at Reba Place Fellowship, teaching and leading both a small group and an extended family household before returning full time to editing and writing.

Neta was born in Winchester, Kentucky, to parents involved in Christian schools as teachers and administrators. Family moves soon took them to Seattle, Washington, where she grew up on the campus of King's Garden, a nondenominational Christian ministry center. Neta attended Multnomah School of the Bible for one year, where she met Dave. She then graduated from Wheaton College with a B.A. in literature. At Reba Place Fellowship, Neta serves on the Women's Council and occasionally teaches.

Together Dave and Neta lead one of Reba's five "clusters" of small groups. A recent book they coauthored (with A. Grace Wenger) is *Witness: Empowering the Church* (Herald Press, 1989).

Beth Landis was born in Sterling, Illinois, in 1957. She graduated from Hesston College (Hesston, Kansas) in 1977 and from Eastern Mennonite College (Harrisonburg, Virginia) with a BSN in 1979. She received her MSN as an adult nurse practitioner from Indiana University.

She worked as a staff nurse on surgical, orthopedic, oncology, medical, and intensive care units in Sterling, Illinois; Peoria, Illinois; and Goshen, Indiana. She taught at Goshen College (Indiana) 1985-1987 and at Indiana University in 1990. She is certified as an adult and gerontological nurse practitioner and has worked as a nurse practitioner in women's health.

Beth is a member of Mennonite Nurses Association and serves on the executive committee as the nurse editor of the *Mennonite Medical Messenger*. She is a member of Mennonite Health Association, American Nurses Association, and Sigma Theta Tau (an international honorary society for nurses).

She is a member of several local committees including Goshen General Hospital Ethics Committee. She has given many presentations on ethics, gerontology, women's health, and skin and wound care. She was a nominee for Indiana Nurse of the Year award in 1989 and is listed in *Who's Who Among American Nurses*.

Beth is a member of Assembly Mennonite Church (Goshen) and is active in sacred dance.